KEYBOARDING
FOR INFORMATION PROCESSING

ROBERT N. HANSON, Ed.D.
Dean, School of Business and Management
Northern Michigan University, Marquette, Michigan

D. SUE RIGBY, Ed.D.
Head, Office Administration and Business Education Department
Northern Michigan University, Marquette, Michigan

Feb 14
F 203) *CLASS*
IN

Pg 28, 29, 30
Tommorow

GREGG DIVISION
McGRAW-HILL BOOK COMPANY

New York	Atlanta	Dallas	St. Louis	San Francisco	Auckland	Bogotá
Guatemala	Hamburg	Johannesburg	Lisbon	London	Madrid	Mexico
Montreal	New Delhi	Panama	Paris	San Juan	São Paulo	Singapore
Sydney	Tokyo	Toronto				

Sponsoring Editor: Audrey S. Rubin
Editing Supervisor: Michael J. Esposito
Production Supervisor: Priscilla Taguer
Design Supervisor: Sheila Granda

Library of Congress Cataloging in Publication Data

Hanson, Robert N   date.
   Keyboarding for information processing.

   1.   Electronic data processing—Keyboarding.
1. Rigby, D. Sue, joint author. II. Title.
QA76.9.K48H36   001.64'42   80-26742
ISBN 0-07-026105-9

   3 4 5 6 7 8 9 0 KPKP 8 9 8 7 6 5 4 3 2 1

ISBN 0-07-026105-9

CONTENTS

PREFACE

What Is Keyboarding?

Keyboarding is the act of inputting information into various types of equipment through the use of a typewriterlike keyboard. The keyboard is the means by which the individual interacts with the equipment. The skill is easy to acquire. All you have to do is put your fingers in the right place and then practice the drills. You will be able to measure your accomplishment as you progress from one page to the next. In no time at all you can develop a skill that will be invaluable to you for the rest of your life.

Who Needs Keyboarding Skills?

Many careers today, from entry-level positions to those in top management, require the use of keyboarding. Tasks that were formerly manual operations have now become automated through the use of computers and other equipment which use a keyboard for data entry. Some of the positions that now require keyboarding skills include the bookkeeper who enters journal transactions into a computer via a keyboard; the records manager who uses the computer terminal keyboard to locate specific documents in the file; the inventory clerk who keeps track of shipments of stock and receipt of new stock via the computer terminal; the airline agent who uses the keyboard for reservations, passenger check-ins, and seat assignments; and the business executive who has a computer terminal on the desk to access current information which will be useful in making managerial decisions. These are but a few of the positions that now require keyboarding skills; the list could continue indefinitely.

The increased use of keyboards on various types of equipment in business, industry, government, and education has created a need to prepare people to use typewriterlike keyboards effectively. In addition, many students need keyboarding skills to interact with computers as part of their academic program. In order to use these keyboards in the most efficient manner, it is important to have basic touch keyboarding skills.

Purpose of the Book
The purpose of this book is to enable a person to develop basic touch keyboarding skill in a minimum amount of time. Specifically, the person who completes this book will be able to:
1. Input alphabetic, numeric, and symbol information on a keyboard.
2. Input numbers on a separate 10-key pad.
3. Keyboard information quickly and accurately.
4. Understand some of the basic vocabulary and concepts used in keyboarding operations for inputting and retrieving information.

How to Use the Book
Keyboarding for Information Processing can be used in a traditional classroom or for individual self-instruction. If you are in a conventional class-

room, your instructor will provide directions as you move through the keyboarding exercises. However, if you are using the book for self-instruction, you can work through the material at your own pace, using the instructions in the left margin.

Always practice the drills in the book as many times as directed, because the only way to develop touch keyboarding skill is through extensive practice.

This book is designed to teach you to keyboard on a typewriter or on some form of text editing equipment. If you are using a machine other than a typewriter, consult the operations manual for specific instructions about the different operations and functions of specific keys.

Checking Your Progress

The Progress Check at the end of each page gives you an opportunity to measure your accomplishment. Type each Progress Check twice—always trying to improve your performance. For example, if you type the Progress Check the first time with 3 errors, try to reduce the number of errors the second time. Or if you type it accurately the first time, try to type it faster the next time. Also, use the Progress Check from the previous lesson as a quick review before you begin a new lesson.

Just remember, keyboarding is a skill, and like any skill—from baseball to tennis—correct practice is the key to success. It's easy and it's fun. Enjoy it!

KEYBOARDING FOR INFORMATION PROCESSING

PART ONE

THE KEYBOARD
ALPHABET, NUMBERS, AND SYMBOLS

```
801    DCL CONTROL CHAR (100) VARYING;
802    DCL CORE FIXED BINARY (31) INIT (50000);
803    DCL DUPSW BIT (1);
804    DCL EOJCARD BIT (1) INIT ('0'B);
805    DCL EOJDISK BIT (1) INIT ('0'B);
806    DCL FIELDS CHAR (50) DEF SORT_FIELDS;
807    DCL LINECNT FIXED BIN (15) INIT (0);
808    DCL MATCH_COUNT FIXED (5,0) INIT (0);
809    DCL MATCHSW BIT (1);
810    DCL MESSAGE CHAR (133);
811    DCL NAME CHAR (30);
812    DCL NO_MATCH_COUNT FIXED (5,0) INIT (0);
813    DCL NO_RECORD_COUNT FIXED (5,0) INIT (0);
814    DCL NOREC BIT (1) INIT ('0'B);
815    DCL NUMBER_CHAR CHAR (7) DEF NUMBER_PIC;
816    DCL NUMBER_PIC PIC 'ZZZZZZ9';
817    DCL PLIRETC BUILTIN;
818    DCL PLISTRA BUILTIN;
819    DCL PRINT_LABEL LABEL;
820    DCL PUNCHSW BIT (1);
821    DCL RC FIXED BINARY (31) INIT (0);
822    DCL RECORD CHAR (70) INIT ('RECORD TYPE=F,LENGTH=80');
823    DCL SAVESSNO CHAR (9);
824    DCL SELECTOR_CARD CHAR (80);
825    DCL 1 SORT_FIELDS,
826        2 FIELDSA CHAR (14) INIT (' SORT FIELDS=('),.
827        2 SS_LOC PIC '99',
828        2 FIELDSC CHAR (34) INIT (',09,A),FORMAT=BI');
```

A keyboard is used to input information into various types of equipment.   Because the location of the alphabet and number keys on most keyboards is similar, the techniques perfected on one machine are easily transferable.

Some keyboards are attached to a visual screen on which the copy appears as each key is depressed.   However, other keyboards are attached to a printer that prints the copy on paper.   These are referred to as hard-copy printers.
   Hard-copy printers use a variety of paper.   For example, tractor-feed machines require special paper that is one continuous sheet with notches on both sides.   The notches fit over pins or sprockets that move the paper forward.   The paper is perforated at

```
601     IDENTIFICATION DIVISION.
602     PROGRAM-ID.     REALSTAT.
603     AUTHOR.         KAY E. BARTON.
604     INSTALLATION.   QUEEN CITY DATA PROCESSING.
605     DATE-WRITTEN.   MAR 11, 1980.
606     DATE-COMPILED.  MAR 19, 1980.
607     SECURITY.       UNCLASSIFIED.
608     *
609     *THIS PROGRAM PRODUCES A MULTIPLE LISTING MASTER FILE,
610     *WHICH IS STORED AS AN INDEXED SEQUENTIAL FILE AND
611     *A REAL ESTATE LISTINGS REPORT WHICH CONTAINS SELECTED
612     *FIELDS FROM THE MULTIPLE LISTING MASTER FILE. ERRORS
613     *IN DATA ARE OUTPUT TO THE EXCEPTION REPORT.
614     *
615     ENVIRONMENT DIVISION.
616     CONFIGURATION SECTION.
617     SOURCE-COMPUTER.            IBM-370.
618     OBJECT-COMPUTER.            IBM-370.
619     SPECIAL-NAMES. C01 IS TO-TOP-OF-PAGE.
620     INPUT-OUTPUT SECTION.
621     FILE-CONTROL.
622         SELECT REAL-ESTATE-TRANSACTION-FILE
623             ASSIGN TO UR-S-SYSIN.
624         SELECT MULTIPLE-LISTING-OUTPUT-FILE
625             ASSIGN TO DA-I-MSTROUT
626             ACCESS IS SEQUENTIAL
627             RECORD KEY IS PARCEL-CODE-MSTROUT.
```

11-inch intervals so that the sheet can be separated into pages and placed in order. Continuous-feed paper is also used with friction-feed machines, which do not require the use of notches to move the paper forward. Instruction manuals for these machines provide detailed directions for paper insertion.

The paper used most frequently in typewriters is a standard $8\frac{1}{2}$ by 11 inches. To insert paper in a typewriter, position the paper guide at the left of the paper and pull the paper bail either forward or up. With your left hand, grasp the paper and put it behind the cylinder against the paper guide. With your right hand, turn the right cylinder knob to draw the paper in.

If the paper is not properly aligned, use the paper release to loosen the paper so you can straighten it. Once the paper is properly aligned, place the paper bail in position. You should leave about $\frac{1}{4}$ inch of paper above the paper bail.

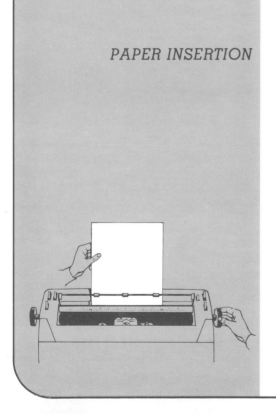

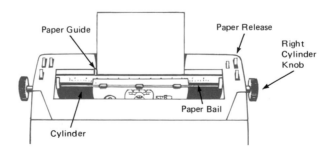

Paper Guide

Paper Release

Right Cylinder Knob

Paper Bail

Cylinder

```
   60 RHOURS = 40.0
      RPAY = RHOURS * RATE
      OTHR15 = 10.0
      OPAY15 = OTHR15 * ORAT15
      OTHR20 = HOURS - 50.0
      OPAY20 = OTHR20 * ORAT20
      OTHR30 = 0.0
      OPAY30 = 0.0
C ******** PRINT OUTPUT
   65 TPAY = RPAY + OPAY15 + OPAY20 + OPAY30
      PAYROL = PAYROL + TPAY
      COUNT = COUNT + 1

      WRITE(6,200)RHOURS,OTHR15,OTHR20,OTHR30,RATE,
     1 ORAT15,ORAT20,ORAT30,RPAY,OPAY15,OPAY20,
     2 OPAY30,TPAY
  200 FORMAT(F5.1,3F8.1,2X,4F9.3,4F10.2,3X,F8.2)
   84 FORMAT('1',T12,'HOURS',T49,'RATE',T86,'PAY SUMMARY',/
     1 T3,'REG',T8,'OT-1.5 OT-2.0 OT-3.0',T35,'R-RATE
     2 O-RATE O-RAT O-RATE REG-PAY OT-PAY OT-PAY OTPAY
     3 TOTAL-PAY',/T45,'(1.5)',T54,'(2.0)',T63,'(3.0)',
     4 T83,'(1.5)',T93,'(2.0)',T103,'(3.0)')
      GO TO 10
  900 AVG = PAYROL/COUNT
      WRITE(6,1000) PAYROL,AVG
 1000 FORMAT(///' TOTAL PAYROLL IS',F10.2,/' AVERAGE
      PAYCHECK IS',F10.2)
      STOP
      END
```

LINE LENGTHS AND MARGINS SETTINGS

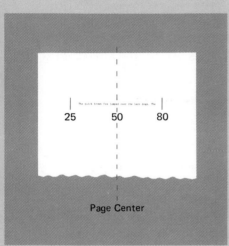

The quick brown fox jumped over the lazy dogs. The

25   50   80

Page Center

COMMON MARGIN SETTINGS
(With the Paper Centered at 50)

Line Desired	Left Margin Stop at	Right Margin Stop at
40 spaces	50 − 20 = 30	50 + 20 + 5 = 75
50 spaces	50 − 25 = 25	50 + 25 + 5 = 80
60 spaces	50 − 30 = 20	50 + 30 + 5 = 85
70 spaces	50 − 35 = 15	50 + 35 + 5 = 90

On most keyboarding equipment, the operator must set the margins to indicate a specific line length. Some electronic machines, however, have preformatted or preset margins that enable the operator to enter data into predetermined fields without manually adjusting the margins. The procedures differ from one piece of equipment to another, so check the instruction manual for the machine you are using.

Since most people who use this text will probably learn to keyboard on a typewriter before transferring their skills to more sophisticated equipment, detailed instructions are provided here for setting margins on a typewriter.

Though it is not always required, copy is generally centered across the paper with a margin on either side. There are three steps in planning the setting of the margin stops on a typewriter.

1. Determine how long a line to use. For example, in this book the direction **Line: 50** means "use a 50-space line."
2. Determine the left margin stop. To do this, subtract half the desired line length from the center of the paper (50), and set the left margin stop at that number on the scale. Example: The setting for a 50-space line would be $50 - 25 = 25$ (left margin).
3. Determine the right margin stop. To do this, add half the desired line (plus 5 extra spaces for the margin bell) to the center of the paper, and set the right margin stop at that number on the scale. Example: The setting for a 50-space line would be $50 + 25 + 5 = 80$ (right margin).

```
100 PRINT "      ELECTRONICS GRADUATE PLACEMENT PROGRAM"
101 PRINT :PRINT
105 PRINT "SELECT ONE OF THE FOLLOWING FUNCTIONS.":PRINT
110 PRINT "      1. ADD NEW ENTRIES"
115 PRINT "      2. PRINT GRADUATES BY DATE"
120 PRINT "      3. PRINT GRADUATES BY NAME"
125 PRINT "      4. PRINT EMPLOYERS BY GEOGRAPHIC REGION"
130 PRINT "      5. PRINT ALL DATA"
140 PRINT
145 PRINT "ENTER FUNCTION NUMBER":INPUT F
155 IF F=0 THEN 999
160 IF F=1 THEN 300
165 IF F=2 THEN 400
170 IF F=3 THEN 500
175 IF F=4 THEN 850
180 IF F=5 THEN 600
200 PRINT "INVALID ENTRY --- TRY AGAIN ! ! ! "
201 GO TO 145
300 REM ADD NEW ENTRIES
302 PRINT :PRINT
304 PRINT
305 PRINT "FIRST LIST THE PROGRAM FROM 1000 TO 10000."
306 PRINT "NEXT ENTER NEW ENTRIES USING NEXT LINE NUMBER."
307 PRINT "END THE FILE WITH THE ENTRY 'DATA 999999'."
308 GO TO 999
400 REM PRINT GRADUATES BY DATE
404 PRINT "ENTER GRADUATION DATA {YYYY} ":INPUT N1
405 PRINT
```

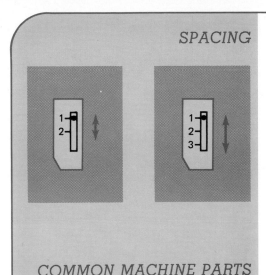

The **line space regulator** controls the amount of space between lines of copy. Set it at 1 for single spacing (no blank lines) or at 2 for double spacing (1 blank line between typed lines). Some machines have settings for $1\frac{1}{2}$, $2\frac{1}{2}$, and 3 spacing.

On those machines which do not have manual line space regulators, it may be necessary to program or "key in" the spacing instructions so that machines with a visual screen or a hard-copy printer will space automatically.

Tabulator   All typewriters and some data-entry equipment have a special mechanism that is used to indent paragraphs or for other operations which require moving the carrier quickly to a desired point without repeatedly striking the space bar. On a typewriter this mechanism is called a **tabulator.**   If you are using a keyboard other than a typewriter, check the instruction manual to determine the name and the location of the key used for this purpose.

Three keys control the tabulator on a typewriter: (1) a **tab-clear key** eliminates tab stops that were previously set, (2) a **tab-set key** sets new stops where needed, and (3) a **tab key** or **tab bar** moves the carrier to those points where the new tab stops are set.

```
305 PRINT "FIRST LIST THE PROGRAM FROM 1000 TO 10000."
306 PRINT "NEXT ENTER NEW ENTRIES USING NEXT LINE NUMBER."
307 PRINT "END THE FILE WITH THE ENTRY 'DATA 999999'."
308 GO TO 999
400 REM PRINT GRADUATES BY DATE
404 PRINT "ENTER GRADUATION DATA (YYYY) ":INPUT N1
405 PRINT
```

Backspace Key   The **backspace key** on a typewriter is designed to move the carrier back one space at a time.   Other keyboards, however, are equipped with a special key which enables the operator to move the carrier back several spaces in one operation.

Correction Key   Many typewriter keyboards have a special **correction key.**   When an error is made, the correction key is used to "back up" to the error.   The incorrect letter is struck again to lift it from the paper.   The correct letter is then typed in the space provided.   These procedures also correct a "stored character" in the memory when an electronic keyboard is used.

   If the machine you are using does not have a correction key, you can correct the errors in typewritten copy three ways: (1) erase the error with a typewriter eraser, (2) cover the error with correction fluid, or (3) lift the error off with coated correction paper.

Margin Release Key   When it is necessary to type beyond the margins set on a typewriter, simply depress the **margin release key.**   Other data-entry keyboards have a special feature which automatically moves the extra letters to the next line.

Shift Lock   Depress the **shift lock** when you want to print in all-capital letters.   If you are using a machine other than a typewriter, be sure to read the instruction manual thoroughly before you begin your practice.

BASIC CODING FORM

PROGRAM_____ DATE_____

PROGRAMMER_____ PAGE_____ OF_____

```
100 PRINT "           ELECTRONICS GRADUATE PLACEMENT PROGRAM
101 PRINT :PRINT
105 PRINT "SELECT ONE OF THE FOLLOWING FUNCTIONS.":PRINT
110 PRINT "      1. ADD NEW ENTRIES"
115 PRINT "      2. PRINT GRADUATES BY DATE"
120 PRINT "      3. PRINT GRADUATES BY NAME"
125 PRINT "      4. PRINT EMPLOYERS BY GEOGRAPHIC REGION"
130 PRINT "      5. PRINT ALL DATA"
140 PRINT
145 PRINT "ENTER FUNCTION NUMBER":INPUT F
155 IF F=0 THEN 999
160 IF F=1 THEN 300
165 IF F=2 THEN 400
170 IF F=3 THEN 500
175 IF F=4 THEN 850
180 IF F=5 THEN 600
200 PRINT "INVALID ENTRY --- TRY AGAIN !!!"
201 GO TO 145
300 REM ADD NEW ENTRIES
302 PRINT :PRINT
304 PRINT
```

Correct posture is one of the most important factors in the development of good keyboarding skills.   Where you sit and how you sit will affect your productivity and your accuracy.

Head erect, turned to face the book.

Back straight, elbows relaxed.

Body centered opposite **J** key, leaning forward.

Feet apart and firmly braced.

The position of your hands is also important.   Your fingers should be slightly curved and positioned as close to the keys as possible—without touching them.

TERMINAL - In general, a device operating remotely via a telecommunication with a central computer or word processing system.*

UNDERSCORE DISPLAY - Underscored characters may be directly displayed or may be indicated by display codes placed before and after material to be underscored on printout.*

WORD PROCESSING - A system of trained personnel, specific procedures, and automated equipment that provides more efficient and economical business communications. Usually involves the transformation of information into readable form.*

WRAPAROUND - Applies to the process of adjusting margins. Word wraparound allows words to be moved from one line to the next to accommodate adjustments, insertions, or deletions; page wraparound will shift words from one page to another.*

---

adapted from
*Word Processing Glossary, International Word Processing Association, Maryland Road, Willow Grove, PA 19090. 1978.

adapted from
**Dartnell's Glossary of Word Processing Terms, The Dartnell Corporation, 4660 Ravenswood Avenue, Chicago, IL 60640. 1977.

The objective of this text is to teach you to keyboard accurately by touch, that is, without looking at the keys. Although you may look at your fingers occasionally when you type the first line of a location drill for a new key, your goal should be to keep your eyes on the copy in the book when you practice. Read and follow all instructions carefully.

The **home-key position** or **home row** refers to those keys on which you place your fingers whenever you keyboard. Although your hands do not actually rest on the home row, they should hover above the keys at all times. As illustrated below, the home-row keys for the left hand are **ASDF** and the home-row keys for the right hand are **JKL;**.

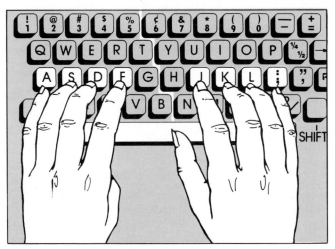

SEARCH - The function of a word processing system which locates specific material on a magnetic tape.**

SHARED LOGIC - Term applied to a type of ~text-editing~ system in which several keyboard terminals simultaneously use the memory and processing powers *of* a single CPU.**

SHIFT - A typewriter key which activates the typing mechanism to print either capital or lowercase characters.**

SPLIT KEYBOARDING - Keyboarding and editing on one unit and playback on another.*

STOP CODE - A reference code recorded on magnetic media which causes the system to stop during printout to allow the operator to perform a procedure such as changing the paper in the printer.*

STORED FORM RECALL/DISPLAY - Ability of a system to store a form (such as text, scale, lines, or a combination of these) and display it upon demand. The operator can then combine the form with new keyboard~ed~ text, print out the completed form, and/or store the form with text or the form and text separately.*

SWITCH CODE - A code which permits switching between media stations of a word processing system, allowing the system to combine such sep~a~rately stored text as an address list with the repeated text of a letter.*

Before you actually learn the home-row keys, however, the first thing to practice is using the space bar and the return key. With all fingers held motionless in home-key position, poise your right thumb about a quarter of an inch above the space bar. Tap the space bar in its center and bounce your thumb off.

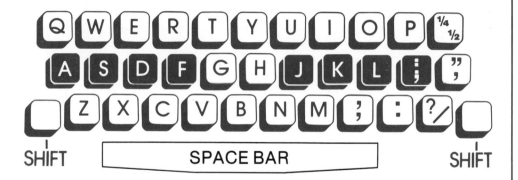

Practice striking the space bar:

Space once [tap the space bar once] . . . **twice** [tap the space bar twice] . . . **once** . . . **once** . . . **twice** . . . **once** . . . **twice** . . . **once** . . . **twice** . . . **twice** . . . **once** . . . **once** . . . **Repeat.**

PLAYBACK, PLAYOUT - The automatic typing out of recorded text.**

PRINTER - In word processing, a device which produces text from recorded material. In some word processing systems, the printer is a separate device wired to the keyboard unit; in others, it is an integral part of the input station.**

PROGRAM - A set of machine instructions for the operation of automated equipment such as computers and word processing systems.**

PROGRAM INSTRUCTION - A code or command which, when keyed into a computer console or word processing typewriter, causes the equipment to respond as desired.** *1 space*

RANDOM ACCESS MEMORY (RAM) - Storage or memory which allows data (such as documents) to be stored randomly and retrieved directly by an address location. The system accesses the addressed material without having to read through intervening data.*

REFERENCE Code *all caps* - An electronically recorded indexing point on a magnetic tape.**

REVISION MODES - The ability of the system to allow the operator selectively to retrieve characters (C), words (W), lines (L), sentences (S), paragraphs (P), or pages at the time of output.*

Practice using the return key:

   In a quick, stabbing motion, (1) extend the little finger of your right hand to the return key; (2) lightly tap the return key, causing the carrier to return automatically; and (3) "zip" the finger back to its home-key position

Space once . . . twice . . . once . . . twice . . . Return! Home! [Fingers on home keys and repeat.]
Space once . . . twice . . . once . . . twice . . . Return! Home!

Practice using the return key until you can do so with confidence. Repeat this drill until you can use the return key without raising your eyes from the printed words.

Line: 50
Spacing: Single

Using the forefingers of each hand (with all other fingers kept in home position), type these three lines. Just tap the keys lightly. Do not space after the last letter in the line before the return.

ALPHABET

Left forefinger on **F** key Right thumb on space bar	}	fff fff ff ff f f ff ff f f
Right forefinger on **J** key Right thumb on space bar	}	jjj jjj jj jj j j jj jj j j
Left forefinger on **F** key Right forefinger on **J** key Right thumb on space bar	}	fff jjj ff jj f j ff jj f j

MEMORY - An integral component of many word processing systems where information is temporarily stored. The memory can act as a buffer for reading or writing to input/output devices, as temporary storage for text entered from the keyboard, and as temporary storage for text being edited or formatted; or it may hold the word processing program.*

Merge *all caps* - To combine, as in the automatic bringing together of information on two tapes into one tape, or onto a document.**

Off-Line *all caps* PRINTING - Ability of a system to print one page of a document while the operator is entering or editing another page of that or any other document.*

OUTPUT - The process of transferring information from internal storage to an external source, such as printing device or storage medium. Also refers to that information itself.*

PARAGRAPH INDENT - A program instruction which enables a word processing unit automatically to indent the first word of a paragraph by a preset number of spaces.**

PINFEED - Pertains to any device for controlling the movement of paper in a machine by engaging pins of the platen or tractor with the holes in the margin of the paper.

HOME-ROW KEYS

```
fff fff jjj jjj fff jjj fff jjj ff jj ff jj f j f
fff fff jjj jjj fff jjj fff jjj ff jj ff jj f j f
fff fff jjj jjj fff jjj fff jjj ff jj ff jj f j f


ddd ddd kkk kkk ddd kkk ddd kkk dd kk dd kk d k d
ddd ddd kkk kkk ddd kkk ddd kkk dd kk dd kk d k d
ddd ddd kkk kkk ddd kkk ddd kkk dd kk dd kk d k d


sss sss lll lll sss lll sss lll ss ll ss ll s l s
sss sss lll lll sss lll sss lll ss ll ss ll s l s
sss sss lll lll sss lll sss lll ss ll ss ll s l s


aaa aaa ;;; ;;; aaa ;;; aaa ;;; aa ;; aa ;; a ; a
aaa aaa ;;; ;;; aaa ;;; aaa ;;; aa ;; aa ;; a ; a
aaa aaa ;;; ;;; aaa ;;; aaa ;;; aa ;; aa ;; a ; a
```

HOME-ROW WORDS

```
add all ask sad lad dad ask asks asks; fall salad
add all ask sad lad dad ask asks asks; fall salad
add all ask sad lad dad ask asks asks; fall salad
```

INPUT - Material entered into a word _or data_ processing system for storage, retrieval, or playback. *

INSERT - A word processing machine function which allows for the introduction of new material within previously recorded ~~material~~ _text_. **

JUSTIFY - To output text with flush left and right margins. *

KEYBOARDING - Inputting information by manipulating a keyboard. Closely resembles "typing" except that "keyboarding" does not have the same connotation of producing printed output. *

LINE NUMBER ACCESS - A means of "addressing" points within prerecorded text through codes which generally correspond to lines of the document numbered sequentially. **

MAGNETIC KEYBOARD - A term used to describe a device for recording alphanumeric characters on a magnetic tape, card, or disc.

MAGNETIC MEDIA - Any of a wide variety of belts, cards, disks, or tapes coated or impregnated with magnetic material, for use with appropriate word processing equipment and on which dictation or keystrokes are recorded and stored. **

Use D finger.

SHIFT   SHIFT

Drills: 2 times each

Progress Check: Type 2 copies of lines 13-14 or take two 1-minute timed writings. To time yourself for 1 minute, use the second hand on a clock or a stopwatch. If possible, have someone else time you.

Goal: Lines 13-14 (12 words)* in 1 minute with 3 or fewer errors. Circle errors. If goal is not achieved, repeat this page.

*5 strokes (including spaces) equals 1 word.

A. LOCATION DRILLS

1 ddd ded eee ddd ded eee ddd ded eee ded dd ee ded
2 ded see see ded fee fee ded lee lee ded dd ee ded
3 ded led led ded fed fed ded fee fee ded dd ee ded
4 ded sea sea ded elk elk ded elf elf ded dd ee ded

B. WORDS

5 see seed seeds seeded seek seeks led fed lee less
6 deed deeds deeded fee fees feed feeds false easel
7 lea fade fades faded feel feels elf self elk elks
8 sell sells dell dells jell jells fell seal sealed

9 ell ells sea seas seals deal deals deaf sake leaf
10 sale sales safe safes jade jaded seek seeks seeds
11 fake fakes faked jell dells desk desks lake lakes
12 elf elk leak leaks leaked keel keels lease leases

C. PROGRESS CHECK

13 fall sale deals; a lad fell; a lass seeks a desk;
14 fake jade;

HARD COPY - Typewritten or printed copy of any description (as opposed to "soft copy" which may be stored on a medium or displayed on a video display but which does not exist on paper).*

Hardware - The machinery of a system, as distinct from the "software" of programs, instructions, and training.*

HOT ZONE - Hyphenation technique in which the operator specifies a fixed- or variable-length zone next to the right-hand margin. A word which will not end before encountering the margin causes typing to halt as soon as the hot zone is entered.*

HYPHEN DROP - A system's ability to drop any hyphen recorded for dividing a word at the end of a line if that word appears in the middle of a line during adjusted play back.

IMPACT PRINTER - a device in which the typing element directly strikes the paper to produce a character or symbol.*

INFORMATION PROCESSING - A term used to describe the integration of data processing, word processing, reprographics, and records management. It includes all business and scientific operations performed by a computer, such as handling, merging, sorting, computing, and editing data.

INKJET PRINTER - A nonimpact printer which sprays ink through an electrostatic field and onto paper to form the intended characters and symbols.**

Use J finger.

SHIFT   SHIFT

Drills: 2 times each

Goal: Lines 13-14 in 1 minute (12 words)* with 3 or fewer errors. Circle errors. If goal is not achieved, repeat this page.

*5 strokes (including spaces) equals 1 word.

A. LOCATION DRILLS

1 jjj juj uuu jjj juj uuu jjj juj uuu juj jj uu juj
2 juj dud dud juj due due juj sue sue juj jj uu juj
3 juj us; us; juj use use juj uke uke juj jj uu juj
4 juj due due juj sue sue juj use use juj jj uu juj

B. WORDS

5 us use uses used useful useless sue sues sued dud
6 dude dudes due dues dusk luff luffs luffed duffel
7 full lull lulls lulled lulu fuel fuels fueled due
8 feud feuds feudal dual duel duels dueled duff use

9 suds sudsless fuss fusses fussed duff duffed kudu
10 auk auks dull dulls dulled duke dukes suede kulak
11 uke ukelele fuddle fuddles fuddled usual sue sued
12 sulk sulks sulked fuse fuses fused uke juke juked

C. PROGRESS CHECK

13 a duke feuds; a lad uses a ukelele; a dude duels;
14 jade sale;

DUAL-PITCH PRINTER - A unit capable of producing text at increments of both 10 and 12 characters per ~~in~~ ** inch.

EDITING - Changes or rearrangements in the text, including reading back, scanning, deleting, substituting, inserting, and reformatting.*

ELEMENT - The removable portion of some character printers which contains the typeface and prints the alphanumeric characters.

EXECUTION INSTRUCTION - A set of ~~basic~~ *elementary* steps (or primitives) carried out by the computer to produce the result specified by the operation code of the instruction.*

FLOPPY (Disk) *all caps* - A circular recording medium providing fast random *a*ccess when used in certain word processing typing systems. Called "floppy" to distingush it from the rigid version often employed in computer memories.**

FORMAT - The arrangement or layout of textual material.**

FORTRAN - FORmula TRANslator--the language for a scientific procedural programming systems.*

FUNCTION KEYS- *+ 1 space* Keys on a keyboard, control panel, or console which activate some machine function other than printing.*

Use F finger.

SHIFT   SHIFT

Drills: 2 times each

Goal: Lines 11-12 in 1 minute (12 words) with 3 or fewer errors. Circle errors. If goal is not achieved, repeat this page.

Omit lines 13-16 if your keyboard prints in capital letters only. Otherwise, to capitalize a letter on the left half of the keyboard:
1. Hold down right shift key with ; finger.
2. Strike letter key.
3. Release shift key and return fingers to home position.

A. LOCATION DRILLS

1 fff fgf ggg fff fgf ggg fff fgf ggg fgf ff gg fgf
2 fgf lag lag fgf jag jag fgf sag sag fgf ff gg fgf
3 fgf dug dug fgf lug lug fgf jug jug fgf ff gg fgf
4 fgf leg leg fgf keg keg fgf egg egg fgf ff gg fgf

B. WORDS

5 lags lagged sags sagged saga jugs jags jagged gad
6 lugs lugged kegs leg legs eggs egged age aged gag
7 adage gale gales gall galled gull gulls glue gage

8 geese glad glade legal legalese glue glued legged
9 juggles juggled guff gulf gas gases gassing edges
10 gaff gaffe fuga fugal fugle fugue fudge sage gags

C. PROGRESS CHECK

11 a jagged edge; a legal sage; a lass juggles eggs;
12 glad gals;

D. LEFT-HAND CAPITALS

13 ;;; A;; A;; ;;; S;; S;; ;;; D;; D;; ;;; A;S; D;D;
14 ;;; Ask Ask ;;; Alf Alf ;;; Ada Ada ;;; Ask; Ada;
15 ;;; See See ;;; Sal Sal ;;; Del Del ;;; See; Del;
16 ;;; Elk Elk ;;; Fae Fae ;;; Gae Gae ;;; Elk; Gae;

CATHODE RAY TUBE (CRT) - An electronic vacuum tube, such as a television picture tube, that can be used to display text and graphic images.*

COBOL - A higher-level, Englishlike, computer-programming language.*

~~CONSOLE - That portion of a computer or word processing system intended~~

CODE - Name given to the specified instruction or action required of a typing unit in playback; a command, e.g., "center," "justify," "stop."**

COMMAND - An instruction to a machine, such as a word processing WP typewriter, to perform a certain action.**

CONSOLE - That portion of a computer or word processing system intended primarily to furnish communication between the human operator and the system by means of lights, switches, and sometimes a typewriter or display.*

CURSOR - The bright, movable dot or arrow on a CRT screen which shows the place on a displayed document for entering new text or making editing changes.**

DEBUGGING - The process of determining the correctness of a computer routine, locating any errors in it, and correcting them. Also the detection and correction of malfunctions in the computer itself.*

Use F finger.

SHIFT   SHIFT

Drills: 2 times each

Note: In all succeeding lessons, type drill lines 2 times each.

Leave 1 space after a semicolon.

Goal: Lines 16-17 in 1 minute (12 words) with 3 or fewer errors. Circle errors. If goal is not achieved, repeat this page.

A. LOCATION DRILLS
1 fff frf rrr fff frf rrr fff frf rrr frf ff rr frf
2 frf fur fur frf far far frf jar jar frf ff rr frf
3 frf err err frf ere ere frf are are frf ff rr frf
4 frf red red frf rug rug frf rag rag frf ff rr frf

B. WORDS
5 errs erred rugs rugged rags ragged raddle dealers
6 rage rages raged raffle raffles jeer jeers jeered
7 reed reef reefed rake rakes raked reel reeled ref
8 raddle raddles lard refer refers referred referee

9 gear gears read reads reader reseed reseeds guard
10 grade large refuel regal regale regard regardless
11 free regress release referral gradual gurgle guru
12 jerk resurge fraud frugal rule ruler dark surreal

C. PHRASES
13 red dress; a rural dealer; a rugged dad referred;
14 gurus are frugal; a large juggler; a free eraser;
15 a user seeks a safer seal; dad releases a refugee

D. PROGRESS CHECK
16 gulls are released; lads dare a reef; large jade;
17 fake desk;

AUTOMATIC PAGINATION — [+ 1space] The ability to take a multipage document and divide it into pages of specified length (in numbers of lines). Often, such ability is joined with the capability to generate page numbers automatically.*

AUTOMATIC REPEAT KEY - A "live" typewriter key such as the underscore which will continue to operate as long as the key is depressed.*

AUTOMATIC TAB MEMORY - Ability of a system to store a format of tab settings to be automatically restored to the tyepwriter at the time of output.*

BACKSPACE CORRECTION - The modes or increments provided by the system during the input process to allow the operator to delete a character (C), [cap] word (W), line (L), sentence (S), paragraph (P), or page.*

BASIC - Beginner's All-purpose Instruction Code. A common time-sharing computer-programming language. Easily learned, it is used for direct communication between teletype units and remotely located computer centers.*

BI-DIRECTIONAL Printer [all caps] - A device capable of printing from right to left as well as from left to right, thus reducing "waste motion" during playout. Also called "reverse printer."**

Use L finger.

Leave 1 space after a period following an abbreviation. Leave 2 spaces after a period at the end of a sentence.

Goal: Lines 16-17 in 1 minute (14 words) with 3 or fewer errors. If goal is not achieved, repeat this page.

A. LOCATION DRILLS

```
1 lll 1.1 ... lll 1.1 ... lll 1.1 ... 1.1 ll .. 1.1
2 1.1 dr. dr. 1.1 sr. sr. 1.1 fr. fr. 1.1 ll .. 1.1
3 lll 1.1 ... lll 1.1 ... lll 1.1 ... 1.1 ll .. 1.1
4 1.1 Dr. Dr. 1.1 Sr. Sr. 1.1 Fr. Fr. 1.1 ll .. 1.1
```

B. WORDS

```
5 Dr. DeSerres keel leaf Fr. lake elk desks Sr. eel
6 Fr. Sell; sale gal gale gull full fall Dr. DeGage
7 Sr. Sue; fell jell sell guesses less gas Dr. Seal
8 Dr. Gale; resurge rudder rude rugged era fr. Sara

9 Sr. Ella; gage gauge ages ageless legal Dr. Sala;
10 Dr. Farr; gears guards radar jar fur rug Sr. Fae;
11 Fr. Drake; fuddle fueled feudal fusses Dr. Fallar
12 Sr. Gerre; useful duffed suede sulk salad Fr. Sal
```

C. SENTENCES

```
13 Dad fed us.  See us.  See Al.  Ask Red.  See Dee.
14 Sue sees us.  Al sees a deer.  A deer sees Della.
15 Della feeds elk.  Reg sells jade.  Dee uses sage.
```

D. PROGRESS CHECK

```
16 Dr. Gerre Drake refused a referral.  Dr. Ella Dee
17 referred Dr. DeSale.
```

ALPHABETIC COMMANDS - Additional instructions to the system, implemented by a code or control key plus alphanumeric key or keys. Such dual-function keys may be marked on the key cap, or the operator may be required to memorize most or all of the alphanumeric command set.*

ALPHANUMERIC - Pertaining to both alphabetic and numeric characters, and ~~and~~ usually including all printable special symbols in the character set.*

AUTOMATIC CARRIAGE - A control mechanism for a typewriter or other listing device that can automatically control the feeding, spacing, skipping, and ejecting of paper or preprinted forms.*

AUTOMATIC CARRIER RETURN - Automatic performance of a carrier return when the last word which will fit on a line is typed. The system generally has a buffer to hold the word currently being typed until the machine judges whether to place the word on the current line or to wrap it onto the next line.*

AUTOMATIC DECIMAL Tab - Automatic alignment of columns of decimal figures on the decimal point. The typist can type numbers without regard for alignment; the system performs the aligning chore.*

AUTOMATIC INPUT UNDERLINING - Ability of the system to cause text to be underscored without the operator having to strike the underscore key for each underlined character.*

Use **J** finger.

SHIFT   SHIFT

Goal: Lines 13-14 in 1 minute (14 words) with 3 or fewer errors. If goal is not achieved, repeat this page.

Omit lines 15-16 if your keyboard prints in capital letters only. Otherwise, to capitalize a letter on the right half of the keyboard:
1. Hold down left shift key with A finger.
2. Strike letter key.
3. Release shift key and return fingers to home position.

A. LOCATION DRILLS

1 jjj jhj hhh jjj jhj hhh jjj jhj hhh jhj jj hh jhj
2 jhj had had jhj hag hag jhj has has jhj jj hh jhj
3 jhj he; he; jhj she she jhj her her jhj jj hh jhj
4 jhj ash ash jhj hue hue jhj hug hug jhj jj hh jhj

B. WORDS

5 here hear hears heard head heads headed hurl hers
6 heel heels heal heals healed healer hedges hedged
7 hale half hard harder hall halls hare hares hadal

8 harsh hassle hassles hassled shake shakes hurdler
9 hugs hugged hugger huge hula hulk hull hulls hush
10 fresh fresher shade shaded share shell shall herd

C. SENTENCES

11 Ed has heard. She shall share. Gar shall laugh.
12 Fred headed here. She had sugar; she had a rash.

D. PROGRESS CHECK

13 Dad held a huge garage sale; Sarah Fae Fuller had
14 heard he had a rake.

E. RIGHT-HAND CAPITALS

15 aaa Jaa Jaa aaa Kaa Kaa aaa Laa Laa aaa JaKa LaHa
16 aaa Use Use aaa Led Led aaa Les Les aaa UaJa HaKa

To produce a corrected hard copy of The Keyboarder's Basic Vocabulary using either an electronic keyboard or a typewriter.

THE KEYBOARDER'S BASIC VOCABULARY

ACCESS - The manner in which files or data are referred to by a computer. In time-sharing, the ability to connect to a free port on the time-sharing system.*

ADDITIONAL CHARACTER - A character which is neither a letter nor a number but a member of a specialized alphabet that includes %, #, and so on, as well as punctuation marks. Specific meanings can be assigned to such a *double space* character to convey special information.
ADDRESS - In computing, the coded representation of the location of a set of data in storage.*

ADJUST - A text-editing feature in which the system automatically adjusts the right-hand margin for insertion or deletion of copy during playback.* ~~Word and sometimes page wrap-around is automatically performed as needed.~~

Use **K** finger.

SHIFT   SHIFT

Leave 2 spaces after a period at the end of a sentence.

Goal: Lines 16-17 in 1 minute (14 words) with 3 or fewer errors. If goal is not achieved, repeat this page.

A. LOCATION DRILLS
1 kkk kik iii kkk kik iii kkk kik iii kik kk ii kik
2 kik air air kik fir fir kik sir sir kik kk ii kik
3 kik kid kid kik did did kik rid rid kik kk ii kik
4 kik dig dig kik jig jig kik rig rig kik kk ii kik

B. WORDS
5 sill dill fill fills filled airs firs kids kidded
6 hid lid lids ire ill ills hire fire sire fig figs
7 rife life gill hill kill his fish dish like likes
8 id ides idea ideal idle ill illegal ire iris isle

9 side ride rile rise risk silk dial sail irregular
10 lied dried fried sisal sigh diehard diesel figure
11 file ride rider riddles ridge rigid field fielder
12 gird rifle digress siege sigh lieu differ diffuse

C. SENTENCES
13 Jill is here; Fred said she is. I like her hair.
14 His eager eagle liked dried figs; she liked fish.
15 He likes his riddles; I like his irregular ideas.

D. PROGRESS CHECK
16 Della said a huge fire like Fred had is a dreaded
17 fear Leslie has had.

Enter the data shown in the columns. If your equipment has tabs, set them for the two columns. If not, use the space bar.

EMPLOYEE WAGE INFORMATION

Employee Name	Identification Number	Hourly Rate
Amman, Donald	3526	5.20
Briggs, Evelyn	2289	6.45
DesJardins, Patrick	4650	5.40
Eppenstein, Herbert	3914	6.70
Lykins, Victoria	3860	5.15
Magadanz, Dennis	2149	6.25
Nelson, Jill	3971	5.35
O'Neill, Austin	2457	6.35
Paterra, Susanne	4039	5.90
Perket, Bond	4127	6.40
Quayle, Alvin	3652	6.75
Robare, Leslie	2379	5.80
Saari, Lydia	4430	6.40
Schlegel, Scott	2675	6.10
Trewhella, Michael	3363	5.95
Wong, Tai-ming	3724	6.55

Proofread your work carefully. If you make more than 2 errors, repeat the drill.

Use **L** finger.

SHIFT   SHIFT

Goal: Lines 16-17 in 1 minute (14 words) with 3 or fewer errors. If goal is not achieved, repeat this page.

A. LOCATION DRILLS

1 lll lol ooo lll lol ooo lll lol ooo lol ll oo lol
2 lol log log lol jog jog lol dog dog lol ll oo lol
3 lol off off lol odd odd lol old old lol ll oo lol
4 lol oar oar lol our our lol oil oil lol ll oo lol

B. WORDS

5 fog hog logs dogs jogs jogged sore fore lore sold
6 rod hod soul foul loud louder sour sours dour ode
7 oak four hour hours soak soaks soaked soar soiled
8 odor oleo oral order hour hours fold gold offside

9 roof roofs roll rolls sofa sore sole shore resold
10 dodge dollar dole doleful door doorsill roar foil
11 soda sodas dough rough rougher fodder folks foods
12 load loaded lodged fools foolish solders soldiers

C. SENTENCES

13 A foolish logger sold loads of logs for a dollar.
14 Hilda jogs; she looks good. She also likes golf.
15 A doleful soldier looked for a deer as he jogged.

D. PROGRESS CHECK

16 Our lodger looked like a real hiker. Fred hauled
17 good logs for fires.

When setting tab stops for columns 2 and 3, leave at least 6 spaces between columns.

NAMES AND SOCIAL SECURITY NUMBERS		
Carrie J. Hyrkas	376 50 2506	
Angela J. Frustaglio	263 28 1836	
Jerome E. Bianco	215 43 1180	
Linda J. Sims	257 32 8055	
James A. Torres	159 16 5990	

BANK ACCOUNT NUMBERS AND DEPOSITS		
43-882-1	478.24	
43-763-6	500.00	
43-874-5	22.70	
43-763-6	814.69	
43-891-9	790.24	

AIRLINE FLIGHT NUMBERS AND PASSENGER NAMES		
342	AJLUNI S	
198	WHITE R	
195	KIELBASCO J	
267	WILKINS M	
479	SWENSON L	

AUTO RENTAL LICENSE NUMBERS AND RENTER NAMES		
MN RJK-315	DE JONG C	
MN LDR-478	BIDEAUX D	
MN RXM-890	DIAZ E	
MN FYD-701	JONES O	
MN BFG-079	MILLIKIN R	

Use **F** finger.

SHIFT   SHIFT

Leave 1 space after a semicolon. Leave 2 spaces after a period at the end of a sentence.

Goal: Lines 16-17 in 1 minute (14 words) with 3 or fewer errors. If goal is not achieved, repeat this page.

A. LOCATION DRILLS

1 fff ftf ttt fff ftf ttt fff ftf ttt ftf ff tt ftf
2 ftf aft aft ftf its its ftf hat hat ftf ff tt ftf
3 ftf too too ftf toe toe ftf the the ftf ff tt ftf
4 ftf let let ftf lot lot ftf got got ftf ff tt ftf

B. WORDS

5 its hit sit sits fit fits rat rats sat raft rafts
6 let lets letter set sets get gets dart darts tart
7 to tore tear take tag tail tailor tale talk taste
8 settle tarts tartar tease terrier rate late dates

9 right sight tight light fight height tasks tassel
10 kit kite rut taught test there their jet set rate
11 tell teller tire strike till tilt stilt teakettle
12 tie tide tigers later titles just adjust tattered

C. SENTENCES

13 Ed liked the red rug at the fair; it is for sale.
14 Al hurt his foot; look at it. His toe does hurt.
15 Those Tigers took titles through a lot of effort.

D. PROGRESS CHECK

16 The four girls adjusted the rig so that it sailed
17 just like the other.

20

KEYBOARDING APPLICATIONS

Line: 60 (Pica)
70 (Elite)
Spacing: Single

NAMES AND ADDRESSES

At this point in the course you should have gained the basic skills for keyboarding the alphabetic letters, numbers, and symbols most commonly found on electronic keyboards. You will now have an opportunity to apply that skill.

Pages 71-84 contain samples of various forms of keyboarding materials that you might encounter in the future. Most important, however, they provide the additional practice needed to master the skill of keyboarding. Pages 85-90, the samples of computer programming materials, are provided for general reference and need not be keyboarded unless they are relevant to your needs.

```
Mr. Craig W. Allenstein
2307 Rosehaven Drive
St. Louis, MO 63141

Mrs. Eunice A. Austin
4518 Pickett Lane
Covington, KY 41011

Mr. William H. Sanchez
758 Vista del Verde
El Cajon, CA 92021

Ms. Dorothy Scarola
4216 Ocean Parkway
Brooklyn, NY 11230
```

Use K finger.

SHIFT   SHIFT

Leave 1 space after a comma.

A. LOCATION DRILLS

1 kkk k,k ,,, kkk k,k ,,, kkk k,k ,,, k,k kk ,, k,k
2 k,k as, as, k,k is, is, k,k us, us, k,k kk ,, k,k
3 k,k to, to, k,k do, do, k,k so, so, k,k kk ,, k,k
4 k,k of, of, k,k if, if, k,k it, it, k,k kk ,, k,k

B. WORDS

5 air, sir, lid, ill, fill, hire, life, sore, gold,
6 jog, odd, hat, get, loud, golf, soil, kits, dart,
7 far, fur, red, rug, keg, leg, egg, jug, rod, she,
8 fig, rig, gill, hill, fire, life, log, dog, oars,

9 hours, golf, foil, good, rafts, hits, dart, seat,
10 fish, kits, soil, hat, gold, life, lid, toe, rig,
11 sat, fat, old, sold, fold, hold, our, sour, four,
12 set, get, let, feet, rid, ride, side, tide, hide,

C. SENTENCES

13 Either Dad, Les, Jill, or Al liked the fish dish.
14 Those golf jokes are so old; shut that radio off.
15 Reed said that Fred, Al, or Rhett sold the desks.

D. PROGRESS CHECK

16 Gilda, Jill, or the rider asked if the rates that
17 I used are too high.

KEYBOARDING FOR INFORMATION PROCESSING

PART THREE

KEYBOARDING APPLICATIONS

Use **D** finger.

SHIFT   SHIFT

Eyes on book!

Quick return at end of line.

Shift quickly for capital letters.

Goal: Lines 16-17 in 1 minute (16 words) with 3 or fewer errors. If goal is not achieved, repeat this page.

A. LOCATION DRILLS

1 ddd dcd ccc ddd dcd ccc ddd dcd ccc dcd dd cc dcd
2 dcd cad cad dcd cod cod dcd cud cud dcd dd cc dcd
3 dcd ice ice dcd ace ace dcd act act dcd dd cc dcd
4 dcd cue cue dcd cut cut dcd cur cur dcd dd cc dcd

B. WORDS

5 cog cogs char chars chat charts cool cools cooled
6 car cat cot coal cart card cook check chill court
7 cots acts cuts core cored cold cash cashed ceases
8 cake cakes coat coats cite cites cited cache curl

9 rice dice lice hack sack rack tack cake case care
10 cage cages deck decks rock rocks lock locks socks
11 lick licks kick kicks cheer cheers chills chilled
12 Cal Carl Carol Cathie Charles Cecil Chuck Charlie

C. SENTENCES

13 The cheerleaders checked their coats at the door.
14 Chuck or Celia cited the checklist for the court.
15 Clifford Daggart cashed four checks at the store.

D. PROGRESS CHECK

16 Get Fredrick, Harold, or Chuck to act as a guide;
17 the others are to check coats.

Enter the numeric data shown. If your equipment has tabs, use them. If not, use the space bar.

BRANCH TELEPHONE CREDIT CARD CHARGES

January and February

Card Number	Branch	January	February
212—668—8601—298—1	3654	198.54	156.32
212—694—3539—340—6	3654	220.31	187.65
212—694—4860—201—5	3654	84.30	63.29
404—822—2413—701—8	5081	315.48	289.67
404—871—2409—228—1	5081	76.42	96.54
404—871—8652—554—0	5081	121.60	146.25
312—227—2920—063—7	4279	79.50	112.80
312—227—2552—631—8	4279	248.36	218.20
312—365—4680—210—3	4279	124.10	87.36
415—541—2249—388—4	6658	347.30	286.45
415—541—3667—495—1	6658	211.24	169.44
415—541—5531—569—7	6658	143.75	156.38
303—917—7018—163—9	8445	235.76	171.40
303—917—6620—190—5	8445	305.10	286.43
303—965—4877—564—1	8445	147.32	204.80

Proofread your work carefully. If you make more than 4 errors, repeat the drill.

Use J finger.

SHIFT   SHIFT

A. LOCATION DRILLS

```
1 jjj  jmj  mmm  jjj  jmj  mmm  jjj  jmj  mmm  jmj  jj  mm  jmj
2 jmj  jam  jam  jmj  ham  ham  jmj  him  him  jmj  jj  mm  jmj
3 jmj  mar  mar  jmj  mat  mat  jmj  mad  mad  jmj  jj  mm  jmj
4 jmj  sum  sum  jmj  gum  gum  jmj  hum  hum  jmj  jj  mm  jmj
```

B. WORDS

```
5 ham hams dam dams ram rams rammed jam jams jammed
6 dim rim mit team seams reams cream stream screams
7 gum gums gummed hums hummed sums summed chum harm
8 mole mold molt foam loam meek meet mood mile mire

9 aim tame same dame fame game lame meat meal might
10 hem mate made mare make male seem deem image mice
11 mile milk time lime come some homes chrome chimes
12 mud muddle much mulch mug madam Mr. Miss Ms. Mrs.
```

C. SENTENCES

```
13 Either Martha or Jack is to go home for the game.
14 Madge is sure her mother might meet some of them.
15 Ms. Miller heard that the class is almost filled.
```

D. PROGRESS CHECK

```
16 Carl, Jack, or the tired old goalie might come to
17 see our last fall soccer game.
```

CREDIT CARD PAYMENTS

Card Number	Amount Due	Amount Paid	Balance
3480–605003–074	365.72	200.00	165.72
3921–480062–663	289.70	289.70	00
4244–671509–388	620.00	400.00	220.00
4588–710032–779	125.50	55.00	70.50
5003–784650–252	728.63	500.00	228.63
5227–490211–335	98.71	35.50	63.21
5559–382106–747	821.38	360.38	461.00
5886–214786–001	434.85	350.50	84.35
6135–000547–333	230.22	230.22	00
6381–675300–221	543.89	250.00	293.89
6661–344429–060	76.23	76.23	00
6885–951110–555	916.97	675.00	241.97
7009–650112–401	340.71	200.00	140.71
7266–887721–395	44.37	44.37	00
8421–111694–266	567.90	250.50	317.40
8510–331565–799	787.34	575.00	212.34

Enter the numeric data shown. If your equipment has tabs, use them. If not, use the space bar.

Proofread your work carefully. If you make more than 4 errors, repeat the drill.

Use ; finger.

SHIFT   SHIFT

To input a character that appears on the top half of a key, depress the shift key on the opposite side of the keyboard.

Leave 1 space after a period following an abbreviation. Leave 2 spaces after a colon.

Goal: Lines 16-17 in 1 minute (16 words) with 2 or fewer errors. If goal is not achieved, repeat this page.

A. LOCATION DRILLS

1 ;;; ;;; ::: ;;; ;;; ::: ;;; ;;; ::: ;;; ;; :: ;;;
2 Dear Al: Dear Jo: Dear Lu: Dear Sir: Dear Em:
3 Mr. El: Dr. Doe: Ms. Reed: Mrs. Mor: Dear Al:
4 Dear Em: To Mr. Ulm: To Mrs. Ulm: To Ms. Seal:

B. WORDS

5 Dear Ed: Dear Katie: Dear George: Dear Jerome:
6 Dear Jo: Dear Celia: Dear Dieter: Dear Trisha:
7 Dear Em: Dear Carla: Dear Jackie: Dear Samuel:
8 Dear Al: Dear Laura: Dear Ardell: Dear Reggie:

9 Dear Sir: Dear Madam: Dear Sir or Madam: Carl:
10 Dear Mr. Camerius: Dear Mr. Ott: Dear Ms. Holm:
11 Dear Dr. Stoddard: Dear Mr. Redford: Dear Gail:
12 Ladies: Dear Ms. Cook: Dear Gar: Dear Mr. Rue:

C. SENTENCES

13 Check some of the detail: make, model, or color.
14 Dear Laura: Some of us do like to see the games.
15 Dear Ms. Heller: Mail those hammers first class.

D. PROGRESS CHECK

16 Dear Harold: Either Al or Harriet must go to the
17 office to get the green folder.

Enter the numeric data shown. If your equipment has tabs, use them. If not, use the space bar.

Proofread your work carefully. If you make more than 4 errors, repeat the drill.

PERSONNEL DATA BASE

Social Security Number	Birth Date	Employment Date	Annual Salary
422–54–0118	06–13–40	09–01–69	22,500
362–76–8859	12–15–49	10–15–73	18,340
291–37–6502	01–17–23	05–07–51	31,870
458–62–9151	11–20–35	07–21–62	23,620
164–80–4436	08–22–43	09–12–68	19,470
238–06–4109	10–30–30	02–28–57	34,800
431–79–3602	05–04–51	07–01–75	14,290
579–32–1048	03–15–39	11–30–65	27,450
310–48–0076	06–04–41	10–12–71	18,050
466–01–5543	07–10–31	04–18–56	30,460
258–44–3809	08–23–53	05–13–75	13,900
538–64–9920	11–22–49	09–18–73	15,850
135–24–6879	01–23–25	11–10–49	36,840
548–37–9922	03–03–51	04–01–76	13,500
260–33–7521	04–19–45	03–24–72	17,840
501–32–6972	10–12–53	10–16–77	13,200

Use S finger.

SHIFT   SHIFT

Goal: Lines 16-17 in 1 minute (16 words) with 2 or fewer errors. If goal is not achieved, repeat this page.

A. LOCATION DRILLS

1 sss sws www sss sws www sss sws www sws ss ww sws
2 sws sow sow sws sew sew sws saw saw sws ss ww sws
3 sws low low sws mow mow sws wow wow sws ss ww sws
4 sws we, we, sws who who sws was was sws ss ww sws

B. WORDS

5 wet wit wig ware wade wage wire waste watch wedge
6 war wag well will walls wiser wager wafer watered
7 row tows crow grows slows wife whale wharf weighs
8 raw jaws wilt wile wilder wider award which woods

9 few sew grew threw throw wrought write wrist wool
10 wreck wreath wrestle would world west weigh witch
11 otherwise willow wildwood width widow whose whole
12 whitewash whistle whereof wheel wheat wailful wed

C. SENTENCES

13 That team is all set for the game with Westfield.
14 Most of the girls will sail across the wide lake.
15 Mr. Willer whistled; the crow flew toward Howard.

D. PROGRESS CHECK

16 Dear Jackie: Sue is right; the team will come to
17 see the four rookies work out.

Enter the numeric data shown. If your equipment has tabs, set them for each column. If not, use the space bar.

Proofread your work carefully. If you make more than 2 errors, repeat the drill.

INVENTORY SHEET

Quantity on Hand	Catalog No.	Unit Price	Value
15	256–310	6.19	92.85
4	982–745	26.58	106.32
12	105–861	10.90	130.80
24	384–520	13.45	322.80
3	99–6427	2.69	8.07
10	81–3590	1.59	15.90
9	18–9285	2.23	20.07
18	76–8666	.57	10.26
2	4012–86	24.87	49.74
25	5786–99	9.64	241.00
1	6201–55	1.69	1.69
5	1746–33	2.36	11.80
11	886–332	3.24	35.64
14	261–009	5.49	76.86
12	555–832	16.97	203.64
2	620–195	10.95	21.90

Use **J** finger.

SHIFT SHIFT

Leave 2 spaces after a colon.

Goal: Lines 16-17 in 1 minute (16 words) with 2 or fewer errors. If goal is not achieved, repeat this page.

A. LOCATION DRILLS

1 jjj jyj yyy jjj jyj yyy jjj jyj yyy jyj jj yy jyj
2 jyj sly sly jyj shy shy jyj sky sky jyj jj yy jyj
3 jyj yes yes jyj yet yet jyj you you jyj jj yy jyj
4 jyj jay jay jyj way way jyj may may jyj jj yy jyj

B. WORDS

5 yes yet you your yours yeast yellow yearly fairly
6 sly shy sky year yacht yield yogurt dearly wildly
7 jay joy way tray weary youth merely surely softly
8 may ray day yard yours yolks freely rarely hardly

9 jelly jolly holly rally tally carry marry roughly
10 try yours holy truly cordially slowly weary carry
11 yak yam merry ferry dairy sorry yardage yardstick
12 Yours truly, Cordially yours, My dear Mrs. Kelly:

C. SENTENCES

13 My team is all ready for the game with West City.
14 Ray may wish to fly to Jersey City with your dad.
15 My dear Ms. Ty: I am sorry to hear of your loss.

D. PROGRESS CHECK

16 Dear Roy: We may wish to see Tracy today; if so,
17 Chuck will get Jeffrey as well.

Use little finger.

REVIEW

If you need additional review, repeat drill C.

A. LOCATION DRILLS

1 6, 5, 4,4 6,6 5,5, 4,,4 6,,6 55,, ,4, 6,6 5,5 ,4,
2 6– 5– 4–4 6–6 5–5– 4––4 6––6 55–– –4– 6–6 5–5 –4–
3 6, 5– 4,4 6–6 5,5, 4–4– 6,,6 5––5 4,4 6–6 ,5, –4–

4 6, 6– 5,5 4,, 6,6– 5,5, ,44, 6,,6 5,5 –4– ,,6 ––5
5 6– 6, 5–5 4–– 6–6, 5–5– –44– 6––6 5–5 ,4, ––6 ,,5
6 6, 5– 4,4 6–6 5,5– 4–4, 6,6, 5–5– ,4, –6– 5,5 4–4

B. REVIEW DRILLS

7 6,5 6,4 4,5 7,69 4,98 8,56 5,69 1,53 2,47 5,8 4,1
8 6–5 6–4 4–5 7–69 4–98 8–56 5–69 1–53 2–47 5–8 4–1

C. NUMBER REVIEW

9   456 426 564 526 650 620 465 1.59 6.42 1.4 5.8 6.3
10 486 413 590 513 680 613 231 7.63 5.73 2.8 6.1 7.2
11 409 450 587 546 679 654 978 8.04 8.01 3.9 8.6 5.3

12 756 789 845 8,907 9,107 156 102 2,560 2.7 306 205
13 723 745 812 8,615 9,863 187 149 2,719 2.0 104 906
14 710 761 803 8,243 9,254 193 157 2,384 2.8 805 704

15 346 3,074 10.64 510.6 9,632 5,791 56–3 2–85 45–61
16 385 3,256 25.08 679.0 8,521 4,872 89–2 4–63 48–72
17 372 3,818 37.90 728.0 7,423 3,890 78–6 7–05 40–96
18 301 3,609 49.01 840.3 6,312 2,708 12–4 1–52 75–68

Use **F** finger.

SHIFT   SHIFT

Goal: Lines 16-17 in 1 minute (18 words) with 2 or fewer errors. If goal is not achieved, repeat this page.

A. LOCATION DRILLS

1 fff fvf vvv fff fvf vvv fff fvf vvv fvf ff vv fvf
2 fvf vie vie fvf vim vim fvf via via fvf ff vv fvf
3 fvf vet vet fvf vat vat fvf eve eve fvf ff vv fvf
4 fvf velvet, fvf valves, fvf vividly fvf ff vv fvf

B. WORDS

5 vim via save cave wave vague vacuum vacate valley
6 vat eve gave have rave vowel vulgar vowels volume
7 vie vet vale vase vast vouch volley voided visual
8 vow vim vary veal veer vivid violet victim vessel

9 strive wives lives veil vise valet valid vaulting
10 levers severe waiver relieve valve vandal various
11 variety vaudeville vault velocity velvet vermouth
12 very verify versatile versus vertical vessel veto

C. SENTENCES

13 Few of those vessels vary with respect to volume.
14 She veered to the right to avoid the hard volley.
15 Several victims rushed to the cave in the valley.

D. PROGRESS CHECK

16 Dear David: I wish Cliff would show Jerry how to
17 serve so he might take two of our games.

Use third finger.

Use third finger.　Use thumb.

Proofread your work. Repeat each line or column once for each error that you made in it.

Work at a steady speed that you can maintain almost without error.

A. LOCATION DRILLS

1	69	69	696	696	6969	6996	6996	6699	969	969	696	969
2	63	63	636	636	6363	6336	6336	6633	363	363	636	363
3	69	63	696	636	6969	6363	6996	6336	696	636	969	363
4	69	93	696	699	6963	6939	9669	3663	696	393	996	339
5	63	39	636	633	6369	6393	3663	6336	636	939	336	993
6	69	63	696	636	6963	6369	6939	6393	969	363	393	939

B. REVIEW DRILLS

7	694	695	947	9698	9491	9592	9497	6989	6929	697	691
8	634	635	347	3638	3431	3532	3437	6383	6323	637	631

A. LOCATION DRILLS

1	6.	6.	6.6	6.6	6.6.	6..6	6..6	66..	.6.	.6.	6.6	.6.
2	40	50	606	404	5050	6006	4004	5500	060	040	505	060
3	6.	40	6.6	505	6.6.	6060	6..6	4004	6.6	505	.6.	060
4	6.	.0	6.6	6..	6.60	6.0.	.66.	0660	6.6	0.0	..6	00.
5	40	0.	505	600	404.	5050	0660	4004	505	.0.	006	..0
6	6.	40	6.6	505	6.60	404.	6.6.	5050	.6.	060	040	.0.

B. REVIEW DRILLS

7	6.5	6.4	3.4	25.6	14.5	74.8	89.0	45.6	10.6	6.8	4.9
8	405	520	6.0	7.04	8.05	9603	1050	24.0	5003	602	409

Use **J** finger.

SHIFT   SHIFT

A. LOCATION DRILLS

1 jjj jnj nnn jjj jnj nnn jjj jnj nnn jnj jj nn jnj
2 jnj nun nun jnj run run jnj sun sun jnj jj nn jnj
3 jnj not not jnj now now jnj nor nor jnj jj nn jnj
4 jnj and and jnj one one jnj can can jnj jj nn jnj

B. WORDS

5 nun run sun fun gun knot know knock train narrate
6 not now nor nod and vane sane onion grain natural
7 van can ran tan fan lane cane needy nerve network
8 one nut end ten ton nice nine noise knife nothing

9 rain train strain narrate narration friend notice
10 gain nutmeat nurse numerate nuisance novel nickel
11 line liner lining name namely nation native taken
12 nose gnat given nature naturally navy naval night

C. SENTENCES

13 The novel was shown on one of those new networks.
14 My friend noticed that the train was not on time.
15 Dear Dr. Crane: The new medicine worked wonders.

D. PROGRESS CHECK

16 Dear Guy: When we see Janice, we will ask her to
17 give Fran and David a list of new names.

Goal: Lines 16-17 in 1 minute (18 words) with 2 or fewer errors. If goal is not achieved, repeat this page.

Use index finger.

Use middle finger.

A. LOCATION DRILLS

1 47 47 474 474 4747 4774 4774 4477 747 747 474 747
2 41 41 414 414 4141 4114 4114 4411 141 141 414 141
3 47 41 474 414 4747 4141 4774 4114 474 414 747 141

4 47 71 474 477 4741 4717 7447 4774 474 171 774 117
5 41 17 414 411 4147 4171 1441 4114 414 717 114 771
6 47 41 474 414 4741 4147 4717 4171 747 141 171 717

B. REVIEW DRILLS

7 475 476 757 7676 7575 7576 7475 7476 4747 457 467
8 415 416 151 1616 1515 1516 1415 1416 4141 451 461

A. LOCATION DRILLS

1 58 58 585 585 5858 5885 5885 5588 858 858 585 858
2 52 52 525 525 5252 5225 5225 5522 252 252 525 252
3 58 52 585 525 5858 5252 5885 5225 585 525 858 252

4 58 82 585 588 5852 5828 8558 5885 585 282 885 228
5 52 28 525 522 5258 5282 2552 5225 525 828 225 882
6 58 52 585 525 5852 5258 5828 5282 858 252 282 828

B. REVIEW DRILLS

7 584 586 841 8686 8484 8481 8586 8587 5858 548 578
8 524 526 241 2626 2424 2421 2526 2527 5252 542 572

Use **S** finger.

SHIFT   SHIFT

Goal: Lines 16-17 in 1 minute (18 words) with 2 or fewer errors. If goal is not achieved, repeat this page.

A. LOCATION DRILLS

1 sss sxs xxx sss sxs xxx sss sxs xxx sxs ss xx sxs
2 sxs six six sxs nix nix sxs fix fix sxs ss xx sxs
3 sxs wax wax sxs tax tax sxs lax lax sxs ss xx sxs
4 sxs fox fox sxs sox sox sxs axe axe sxs ss xx sxs

B. WORDS

5 six nix fix ox oxen axiom exact exalt excel exert
6 wax tax lax exile exist oxide extra exceed excuse
7 fox vex axe exit excess excise excite extravagant
8 mix examine excuse exhale exhort extend extension

9 oxygen examine exclaim exclude execute exaggerate
10 exhaust extinct extreme axillary excellent excess
11 excavate exchange exercise exterior extraordinary
12 exclusion executive exultation exonerate external

C. SENTENCES

13 Lex will find an excuse for failing the tax exam.
14 The executives execute their exercises very well.
15 There was extreme excitement when Rex went ahead.

D. PROGRESS CHECK

16 Dear Rex: Extend my thanks to Alan Dixon for the
17 extraordinary and extravagant gesture.

HOME-KEY POSITION FOR THE NUMERIC KEYPAD

Use index finger for **4**, middle finger for **5**, and third finger for **6**.

You may enter the numbers by line or column. Strike the enter key after each entry.

Proofread your work. Repeat each line or column once for each error that you made in it.

The home-row keys are the 4, 5, 6, and , keys. The index finger strikes the 4, the 7, and the 1. The middle finger strikes the 5, the 8, and the 2. The third finger strikes the 6, the 9, the 3, and the . key. The little finger strikes the , key, the - key, and the enter key. The thumb strikes the 0 key.

A. LOCATION DRILLS

1 44 55 444 666 4444 5555 4444 6666 444 555 444 666
2 55 44 555 666 5555 4444 5555 6666 555 444 555 666
3 66 44 666 555 6666 4444 6666 5555 666 444 666 555

4 45 46 454 545 4546 5464 4554 6446 454 646 445 664
5 54 56 545 656 5456 4565 5445 6556 545 656 554 665
6 64 65 646 565 6465 4656 6446 5665 646 565 664 556

B. REVIEW DRILLS

7 456 445 556 4455 5566 6655 4556 5664 5464 654 546
8 654 664 445 5566 6644 5544 5664 6445 6546 546 465
9 546 556 664 6644 4455 4466 6445 4556 4546 465 654

Use ; finger.

SHIFT   SHIFT

Goal: Lines 16-17 in 1 minute (18 words) with 2 or fewer errors. If goal is not achieved, repeat this page.

A. LOCATION DRILLS

1 ;;; ;p; ppp ;;; ;p; ppp ;;; ;p; ppp ;p; ;; pp ;p;
2 ;p; lap lap ;p; nap nap ;p; map map ;p; ;; pp ;p;
3 ;p; pin pin ;p; pen pen ;p; pan pan ;p; ;; pp ;p;
4 ;p; pox pox ;p; pot pot ;p; put put ;p; ;; pp ;p;

B. WORDS

5 pin pen pan pun put spot jump scrap scrape postal
6 sip dip rip lip tip wrap spin apply poster tiptoe
7 lap nap map rap tap dump span cheap oppose supply
8 hop top mop cap nap trap post taper prefer limped

9 paper applaud application grasp clasp please snap
10 past present approve preference pony trap tapioca
11 chip lump appoint tap tape topcoat print printing
12 prince princess topside topsail trip trap printer

C. SENTENCES

13 Palmer applied for that position as a programmer.
14 Paul preferred to purchase a new supply of paper.
15 The proud prince took a trip to see the princess.

D. PROGRESS CHECK

16 The new printing process used at the plant is the
17 preferred method used in the corporation.

NUMERIC KEYPADS

Some computer terminals have a separate numeric keypad located to the right of the regular keyboard. This separate keypad is used when large amounts of numeric data are entered.

The separate keypad enables the operator to enter numbers quickly in adding-machine fashion. All number keys, the minus or hyphen key, the comma key, and the period key have the same function as the corresponding keys on the main keyboard.

The enter key has a similar function as the return key on the main keyboard.

Use **F** finger.

SHIFT   SHIFT

Goal: Lines 16-17 in 1 minute (18 words) with 2 or fewer errors. If goal is not achieved, repeat this page.

A. LOCATION DRILLS

1 fff fbf bbb fff fbf bbb fff fbf bbb fbf ff bb fbf
2 fbf fob fob fbf job job fbf rob rob fbf ff bb fbf
3 fbf bud bud fbf but but fbf bug bug fbf ff bb fbf
4 fbf be, be, fbf box box fbf by, by, fbf ff bb fbf

B. WORDS

5 fob job rob sob robe probe rubber trouble abandon
6 bud but bug bus boat above double dribble subject
7 box bog bow bob bear brisk barrel bracket subhead
8 bat bad ban bar bell brick stable subside brother

9 barn barge battle gabardine because suitable bell
10 back debit carbon carburetor become business bank
11 bird ebony debate hybrid behalf breathless bypass
12 boat gable brother brown building probably submit

C. SENTENCES

13 The business at the banks will probably be brisk.
14 Bev said that her brother may buy that blue bell.
15 If Bill buys the boat, the gray bus will be sold.

D. PROGRESS CHECK

16 Dear Ralph: Please excuse my delay in making the
17 adjustment of the bill Woodrow received.

KEYBOARDING FOR INFORMATION PROCESSING

PART TWO

THE 10-KEY NUMERIC PAD

Use ; finger.

SHIFT   SHIFT

Use ; finger.

Leave 2 spaces after a question mark.

Goal: Lines 7-8 in 1 minute (18 words) with 2 or fewer errors. If goal is not achieved, repeat this page.

A. LOCATION DRILLS

1 ;;; ;/; /// ;;; ;/; /// ;;; ;/; /// ;/; ;; // ;/;
2 ;/; his/her ;/; him/her ;/; we/they ;/; ;; // ;/;

B. WORDS AND SENTENCES

3 / his/her him/her we/they yes/no and/or now/later
4 There are two kinds of current: the a/c and d/c.
5 There is no charge. Please mark the invoice n/c.
6 They expected each keyboarder to do his/her best.

A. LOCATION DRILLS

1 ;;; ;/; ;/?; ;??; ;;; ;/; ;/?; ;??; ;?; ;; ?? ;?;
2 ;/; ;?; who? who? ;/; ;?; how? how? ;?; ;; ?? ;?;

B. WORDS AND SENTENCES

3 Who? How? Why? Where? When? What? How many?
4 Who is there? Why does it work? Where is Janet?
5 When does the office open? It opens around noon.
6 Did you say that not all keyboards are identical?

C. PROGRESS CHECK

7 Did Jane give yes/no answers on the test covering
8 the text? Paul bypassed the final exam.

SYMBOL REVIEW

Line: 60
Spacing: Single

#

$

%

```
ddd ded de3 de3 d3d d3# d#d d#d in #1 and #2 and #3 and #4.
fff frf fr4 fr4 f4f f4$ f$f f$f in $1 and $2 and $3 and $4.
fff f5f f5f f5% f5% f5% f%f f%f in 1% and 2% and 3% and 4%.
```

&

( )

,

```
jjj juj ju7 ju7 j7j j7& j&j j&j in A&P, in T&T, and in S&D.
lll lo9 lo( l(l ;;; ;p0 ;0) ;); in (a), in (b), and in (c).
;;; ;'; ;'; ;'; ;;; ;'; ;'; ;'; in it's, hadn't, and can't.
```

"

-

*

```
;;; ;'; ;'; ;'" ;"; ;"; ;'; ;"; in "Well," he said, "Well."
;;; ;p; ;p- ;p- ;-; ;p; ;-; ;-; in one-half and one-fourth.
kkk kik ki8 ki8 k8k k8* k*k k*k in Smith* and in Perkins.**
```

/ and ?

½ and ¼

```
;;; ;p; ;p- ;p- ;-; ;-_ ;_; ;_; in 11 and 12 and 13 and 14.
;;; ;/; ;/; ;;; ;/? ;/? ;/; ;?; in him/her?  And they/them?
;;; ;½; ;½; ;;; ;¼ ;¼ ;½; ;¼; in 1¼ and 1½ and 2¼ and 2½.
```

¢ and @

```
jjj jy6 j6¢ j¢j sss sw2 s2@ s@s as in 21 @ 20¢ or 66 @ 15¢.
```

Do these drills if your machine has =/+ and 1/! keys.

```
;;; ;½; ;½= ;½= ;=; ;=; ;½; ;=; as in 1 plus 1 = 3 minus 1.
;;; ;½= ;=; ;=+ ;=+ ;+; ;=; ;+; as in 100 + 100 = 150 + 50.
aaa aqa aql ala al! a!a ala a!a as in 1! or 2! or 3! or 11!
```

Use **A** finger.

SHIFT   SHIFT

A. LOCATION DRILLS

1 aaa aza zzz aaa aza zzz aaa aza zzz aza aa zz aza
2 aza zip zip aza zig zig aza zag zag aza aa zz aza
3 aza zoo zoo aza zed zed aza zee zee aza aa zz aza
4 aza buzzers aza zestful aza dizzily aza aa zz aza

B. WORDS

5 zip zig buzz zest size dizzy amaze zealot zealous
6 zoo zed jazz lazy zany dozen zippy zenith zoology
7 zag zig doze zone zing zebra dozed zephyr zillion
8 zee zap zero zinc zoom zingy zeros zigzag agonize

9 civilize civilization authorized dramatize zinnia
10 zither memorize bizarre zipper criticize zucchini
11 alphabetize categorized zoology zoological frenzy
12 bazaar zombie minimize maximize zenith capitalize

C. SENTENCES

13 Buzz was amazed at the size of the zoology class.
14 The size of the jazz band could be about a dozen.
15 She saw a bizarre frenzy of activity at a bazaar.

D. PROGRESS CHECK

16 Dear Victor: Would your five groups like to hear
17 our newest jazz albums? How about next Thursday?

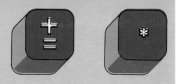

Use ; finger. Use **K** finger.

SHIFT   SHIFT

Read the paragraph and then keyboard a copy.

Goal: Lines 14-16 in 1 minute (30 words) with 2 or fewer errors. If goal is not achieved, repeat this page.

A. LOCATION DRILLS

1 ;;; === ;;; === ;=; ;=; a = 2 b = 4 c = 16 d = 35
2 ;=; ;+; ;=; ;+; ;=; ;+; 7 + 9 8 + 2 3 + 10 1 + 48
3 k8k k*k k8k k*k k8k k*k Rigby* Rubin* and Hanson*
4 ;=; ;+; k*k ;=; ;+; k*k 2 + 4 = 6 and 6 + 7 = 13*

B. SENTENCES

5 He reported that A = 95 or more and B = 88 to 94.
6 They said to total a + b, then b + c, then c + d.
7 Jason Wilson* used an asterisk (*) in a footnote.

C. KEYBOARDING CONCEPTS: *Execution Instructions*

8   Execution instructions are a series of basic
9 instructions that activate the computer to pro—
10 duce the output identified in a specific computer
11 program. The terms "execute" and "run" are used
12 to command the computer to carry out these in—
13 structions.

D. PROGRESS CHECK

14 That book by Kafer* contains office—like problems
15 for developing production typewriting skill. You
16 will be quite amazed at the extra jumps in speed.

Use **A** finger.

SHIFT   SHIFT

Goal: Lines 16-17 in 1 minute (20 words) with 2 or fewer errors. If goal is not achieved, repeat this page.

A. LOCATION DRILLS

1 aaa aqa aqqa aqqa aaa aqa aqqa aqqa aqa aa qq aqa
2 aqa aqa quit quit aqa aqa quip quip aqa aa qq aqa
3 aqa aqa quiz quiz aqa aqa quay quay aqa aa qq aqa
4 aqa quick quickly aqa quiet quietly aqa aa qq aqa

B. WORDS

5 quip quit quite quiet quick quell acquit eloquent
6 quiz quad quail quart queen quota quarry acquaint
7 quid quay quake quill quash quote quench bequeath
8 quad quip qualm quilt squaw squad torque quantity

9 acquire quotation quadruple quarantine quintuplet
10 acquittal acquaintance acquisition bequest unique
11 quality qualify quarrel quarter quarterly quintet
12 quartile question questionnaire quickly liquidate

C. SENTENCES

13 He quite quickly wrote the equation for the quiz.
14 The quarterback questioned a call in the quarter.
15 He gained an eloquent style in his voice quality.

D. PROGRESS CHECK

16 Dear Susan: Both the quiz and the exam proved to
17 be just as difficult as the teachers had claimed.

Use **J** finger. Use **S** finger.

SHIFT   SHIFT

Read the paragraph and then keyboard a copy.

Goal: Lines 15-17 in 1 minute (30 words) with 2 or fewer errors. If goal is not achieved, repeat this page.

A. LOCATION DRILLS

1 j6j j¢j j6j j¢j 3¢ 119¢ 49¢ 25¢ 68¢ 72¢ 17¢ 84¢ 31¢
2 j6j j¢j j6j j¢j 5¢ 116¢ 10¢ 20¢ 55¢ 73¢ 64¢ 98¢ 40¢
3 s2s s@s s2s s@s @ 21¢ @ $1 @ 67¢ @ $1.18 @ $45.39
4 s2s s@s s2s s@s @ 98¢ @ 72¢ @ $3 @ $5.40 @ $91.60

B. SENTENCES

5 We got 6 orders at 16¢, 6 at 16½¢, and 12 at 17¢.
6 Order 12 boxes @ 86¢ and another 144 boxes @ 75¢.
7 Try to get 10 @ 28¢, 39 @ 47¢, and 56 @ 56¢ each.

C. KEYBOARDING CONCEPTS: *Off-Line Printing and Split Keyboarding*

8   Many systems have the ability to print one
9 page of a document while at the same time another
10 page is being entered or edited by the keyboard
11 operator. Some systems also have split-keyboard-
12 ing capabilities enabling the operator to key-
13 board or edit on one terminal and play back on
14 another.

D. PROGRESS CHECK

15 Jay was quite excited to learn that he could pur-
16 chase 10 knives @ 99¢ each or 200 @ 79¢ each, but
17 he had no money when he got to the discount shop.

Use **;** finger for hyphen.

SHIFT   SHIFT

A. LOCATION DRILLS

1 ;;; ;p; ;p-; ;--; ;;; ;p; ;p-; ;--; ;-; ;; -- ;-;
2 ;p- ;-; blue-gray ;p- ;-; one-third ;-; ;; -- ;-;
3 ;p- ;-; one-fifth ;p- ;-; part-time ;-; ;; -- ;-;
4 ;p- ;-; left-hand ;p- ;-; one-sixth ;-; ;; -- ;-;

B. WORDS

5 one-third blue-gray well-to-do clear-cut stand-in
6 left-hand one-fifth forty-one secretary-treasurer
7 one-sixth duty-free clerk-typist do-it-yourselfer
8 part-time forty-six up-to-date low-risk nine-week

9 pay-as-you-go out-of-town high-ranking short-term
10 double-spaced long-range high-grade old-fashioned
11 eight-year-old tax-exempt two-week off-the-record
12 well-known cross-examine ten-story fire-resistant

C. SENTENCES

13 Forty-three clerk-typists work at part-time jobs.
14 Well-known lawyers cross-examined the ex-convict.
15 Short-term loans are available to out-of-towners.

D. PROGRESS CHECK

16 As you know, five huge squads will practice twice
17 a week next year; those judges may be amazed too.

Use **F** finger. Use **A** finger.

SHIFT   SHIFT

Leave 2 spaces after an exclamation point.

Read the paragraph and then keyboard a copy.

Goal: Lines 15-17 in 1 minute (30 words) with 2 or fewer errors. If goal is not achieved, repeat this page.

A. LOCATION DRILLS

1 f4f f$f f4f f$f f4$f Pay $4 or $14 or $41 or $44.
2 f4f f$f f4f f$f $10 $29 $38 $47 $56 $90 $123 $456
3 ala a!a ala a!a No! Fire! Look out! Fantastic!
4 ala a!a ala a!a Wow! Yes! Hurry! You, get out!

B. SENTENCES

5 May thought that $14 was about $4 or $5 too much.
6 No! It just can't be true! How could it happen!
7 Fantastic! I'll buy it for $67 less $9 discount!

C. KEYBOARDING CONCEPTS: *Hot Zone*

8   The hot zone on magnetic storage equipment
9 is a hyphenation technique used to control a
10 variable length zone at the right margin. When a
11 document is played back, this feature allows the
12 machine to decide to start a new line or to halt
13 so that the operator can make a hyphenation
14 decision.

D. PROGRESS CHECK

15   Congratulations! Both judges will award the
16 $50 prize to your computer team for that event in
17 which Frank Dickson quite honestly did not excel.

ALPHABET REVIEW

If you are consistently reaching 20 words a minute on the Progress Checks with 2 errors or less, you may omit this review section and go on to page 43. However, this section is strongly recommended for reinforcing key locations and improving accuracy (pages 36-40), as well as for building speed (pages 41-42).

Line: 60
Spacing: Single
Drills: 2 times each

KEY LOCATION REVIEW

HOME ROW

1 a;sldkfjghfjdksla; a;sldkfjghfjdksla; a;sldkfjghfjdksla; a;
2 asdfg ;lkjh gfdsa hjkl; asdfg ;lkjh gfdsa hjkl; asdfg ;lkjh

HOME AND THIRD ROW

3 frfrf jujuj fgfgf jhjhj deded kikik swsws lolol aqaqa ;p;p;
4 a;qpa; slwosl dkeidk fjrufj ghtygh fjrufj dkeidk slwoslqpa;

HOME AND FIRST ROW

5 fbfbf jnjnj fvfvf jmjmj dcdcd k,k,k sxsxs l.l.l azaza ;/;/;
6 a;z/a; slx.sl dkc,dk fjvmfj fjbnfj dkc,dk slx.sl a;z/a;z/a;

ALL ROWS OF LETTERS

7 aqaza ;p;/; swsxs lol.l dedcd kik,k frftfgfbfvf jujyjhjnjmj
8 a;qpa;z/a; slwoslx.sl dkeidkc,dk fjrufjvmfj fjtyfjghfj bnfj

Use **D** finger. Use **F** finger.

SHIFT   SHIFT

Read the paragraph and then keyboard a copy.

Goal: Lines 14-16 in 1 minute (28 words) with 2 or fewer errors. If goal is not achieved, repeat this page.

A. LOCATION DRILLS

1 d3d d#d d3d d#d #3 #67 #54 #120 #890 10# 29# 387#
2 d3d d#d d3d d#d #4 #56 #90 #123 #678 45# 28# 739#
3 f5f f%f f5f f%f 4.5% or 5% or 5.5% or 6% and 6.5%
4 f5f f%f f5f f%f 75% or 8% or 8.5% and 9% and 9.5%

B. SENTENCES

5 Pack orders #105 and #286 in lots of 39# and 47#.
6 She wanted 15% interest, but I would pay only 5%.
7 Orders #10 and #28 made up over 39% of the total.

C. KEYBOARDING CONCEPTS: Stop Function

8   The stop key is a function key that inserts
9 stop instructions or halts action directly. If
10 instructions are programmed, the system will stop
11 at a specified point during the output process.
12 This is done to allow the operator to insert man—
13 ually specific information such as an address.

D. PROGRESS CHECK

14 James and/or Frank were quick to observe that the
15 crop was excellent. The hybrid #4 had large-size
16 kernels with only 5% moisture by weight.

INDIVIDUAL LETTER DRILLS

Select the letters with which you have difficulty and practice those lines. As you practice, (1) keep your wrists quiet, (2) tap the keys lightly, and (3) use an even rhythm.

A   alarm awake again arena amaze mania amass Allan Alamo Carla
B   abbot cabby bible bulbs bobby nabob tubby Barby Abbey Debby
C   comic check crick cache coach crack civic cycle Chick Chuck
D   dozed dodge dread dandy faded aided ended ceded David Daddy

E   level erred elite every elect exert eager defer Elvis Elgin
F   stuff bluff staff affix stiff taffy affix forty Duffy Cliff
G   gorge aging gauge gouge foggy soggy girls grape Peggy Gregg
H   hatch thigh shush harsh check might other shall Heath Helen

I   civic livid limit idiom vivid finis icing Miami India Dixie
J   joint jelly judge jolly enjoy joker juice Jacob James Jerry
K   kyack knock kulak khaki kinky kapok kayak Kathy Karen Kodak
L   alley local lilac legal label libel lowly ladle Lloyd Laila

M   memos maxim manor month mummy mumps mamma comma Mommy Mamie
N   annex ninth linen onion union nylon unpin nouns Ronny Nonny
O   rotor ozone solos odors polio color moose proof roost scoop
P   puppy piped plump pupil poppy pipes apply peppy sappy happy

Use ; finger.

SHIFT   SHIFT

Read the paragraph and then keyboard a copy.

Goal: Lines 15-17 in 1 minute (28 words) with 2 or fewer errors. If goal is not achieved, repeat this page.

A. LOCATION DRILLS
1 ;'; ''' ;'; ''' I'm that's we'll isn't he's dog's
2 ;'; ''' ;'; ''' Jane's Bob's Terri's Don's Anne's
3 ;'; ;"; ;'; ;"; "Well," "Hello, Brian," "hurried"
4 ;'; ;"; ;'; ;"; "mewed": "Who, me?" "In reply,"

B. SENTENCES
5 We can't find Johnny's cap. Help us look for it.
6 Joy "hurried"; so did I. He "mewed": "Who, me?"
7 His "bite" isn't as bad as his "growl," I'm told.

C. KEYBOARDING CONCEPTS: *Automatic Margins*
8   Once margins have been set, they will adjust
9 automaticaly by pressing a special function key
10 when information is inserted in or deleted from
11 the text. Words move up to the preceding line or
12 down to the next line to accommodate these ad-
13 justments. If a hyphen was used, it will be
14 dropped.

D. PROGRESS CHECK
15 He doesn't question whether the new tax laws will
16 help to "maximize" revenue; his feelings are that
17 they will just come back with more laws.

Q	quail	query	pique	quilt	quite	equip	quake	equal	Quinn	Queen
R	rover	refer	recur	error	arrow	brier	drier	prior	Ralph	Perry
S	sales	socks	loses	slash	sense	suits	sizes	guess	Texas	Susan
T	total	truth	trout	trait	taste	teeth	title	tooth	Dotty	Terry

U	usual	usury	usurp	issue	truly	would	about	could	Trudy	Louis
V	vista	vague	verve	every	never	visit	halve	heavy	Verna	Vicky
W	whoop	where	wharf	swish	allow	while	renew	worth	Wally	Wayne
X	Maxim	sixes	extra	exact	sixty	vexed	waxed	index	Dixie	Xerox

Y	youth	dryly	shyly	slyly	mayor	study	style	yield	Young	Royal
Z	zebra	ozone	amaze	fizzy	dozen	dozed	razor	prize	Ozzie	Lizzy

ALPHABET
REVIEW

Vicky placed one dozen jugs from Iraq on the waxy tabletop.
Paul reviewed the subject before giving Max and Kay a quiz.
With all kinds of gripes, Buzz rejects every required exam.

Queen Judy gave my boy an exciting gold prize for his work.
Rex amazed Jack by pointing quickly to five of the answers.
Ozzie can adjust my diving board for quick, flexible whips.

Use J finger.   Use ; finger.

Read the paragraph and then keyboard a copy.

Goal: Lines 15-17 in 1 minute (28 words) with 2 or fewer errors. If goal is not achieved, repeat this page.

A. LOCATION DRILLS

1 j7j j&j j7j j&j Jones & Sons Brown—Carnahan & Co.
2 j7j j&j Baxter & Jones Kerwin, Stevens, & Company
3 ;—; ;_; ;—; ;_; <u>three</u> tapes <u>not</u> going <u>left</u> signal
4 <u>Principles of Data Processing</u> and <u>Word Processing</u>

B. SENTENCES

5 Write to Dodd & Co., Hess & Park, and Wold & Son.
6 I have <u>not</u> read that new book, <u>Paying for Supper</u>.
7 Consler & Margrif are publishing <u>Word Processing</u>.

C. KEYBOARDING CONCEPTS: Deletion

8   On text—editing equipment, a keyboard opera-
9 tor can delete copy by striking a special func-
10 tion key. This key permits removal of any por-
11 tion of previously recorded information from the
12 system without entering new data. The line
13 length will adjust automatically to allow for the
14 deletion.

D. PROGRESS CHECK

15 Dear Mrs. Klein: Fox & Young will <u>not</u> revise the
16 quotations which you categorized as being much in
17 excess of prices you feel are justified.

1 Five or six big jet planes zoomed quickly by the new tower.
2 Jack quietly gave some dog owners most of his prize boxers.
3 The expert quickly noted five bad jewels among the zircons.

4 Hal was quick to give us extra pizza and juice for my boys.
5 My fine ax just zipped through the black wood quite evenly.
6 Roxie picked all the amazing yellow jonquils by the cavern.

7 Jane gave my excited boy quite a prize for his clever work.
8 I was quickly penalized five or six times by Major Higgins.
9 Jacques picked five boxes of oranges while Diz stayed home.

10 Kay bought five or six cans to award as equal major prizes.
11 Poor Jack was vexed about my long and quite hazy falsehood.
12 The very next question emphasized the growing lack of jobs.

Goal: Lines 13-14 in 1 minute (20 words) with 2 or fewer errors. If goal is not achieved, repeat this page.

PROGRESS CHECK

13 The top executives of the Jupiter Company will be amazed by
14 how quickly Roger can audit the ledgers.

Use L finger.   Use ; finger.

SHIFT   SHIFT

Read the paragraph and then keyboard a copy.

Line: 50
Spacing: Single

Goal: Lines 14-16 in 1 minute (26 words) with 2 or fewer errors. If goal is not achieved, repeat this page.

SYMBOLS

A. LOCATION DRILLS
1 191 9(1 191 1(1 and ;0; ;); ;0; ;); (1) (10) (11)
2 (10) (1100) (1290) (2389) (13570) (34578) (45678)
3 (79 pounds) (548 bushels) (320 acres) (16 inches)
4 (John, that is) (ten dollars) (1) (2) (3) (a) (b)

B. SENTENCES
5 The captain (John, that is) caught the long pass.
6 Bob is (1) tall, (2) dark, and (3) very handsome.
7 They need (a) six invoices and (b) six envelopes.

C. KEYBOARDING CONCEPTS: *Automatic Centering*
8   Some magnetic media keyboards are equipped
9 to center copy automatically between the margins,
10 between designated points, or over a tabulated
11 column. When the center function key is pressed,
12 it makes the system center the preceding copy, or
13 in some systems, the next segment of copy.

D. PROGRESS CHECK
14 She received authorization (by telephone) to join
15 a quiet graphic display printer to that computer.
16 I expect it in about 14 weeks.

1 Max had a zest for quiet living and placed work before joy.
2 Zeke quietly placed five new jumping beans in the gray box.
3 Six jumbo elephants quickly moved the wagon from the blaze.

4 Jack found the gravel camp six below zero quite a few days.
5 Ken promptly requested five dozen jugs of wax for the club.
6 Jasper quietly viewed the next game of checkers with Buzzy.

7 He quickly trained a dozen brown foxes to jump over a gate.
8 Jacqueline was vexed by the folks who got the money prizes.
9 I quickly explained that few big jobs involve many hazards.

10 Jo saw six big packs of cards and seized them very quickly.
11 May brought back five or six dozen pieces of queer jewelry.
12 The very next question emphasizes the growing lack of jobs.

Goal: Lines 13-14 in 1 minute (20 words) with 2 or fewer errors. If goal is not achieved, repeat this page.

PROGRESS CHECK

13 The Sioux fans were amazed as the Wildcats adjusted and ran
14 up very quick goals to win the big game.

6

j 6 j6 16 61 166 661 1661 6616 6161 1616 166 661 16 61 6jj6
Marilyn has 6 brothers, 6 sisters, 16 uncles, and 16 aunts.
666 j6j6j j6j The 66 tests were for 66 girls in 66 classes.
On January 16, 66 houses and 61 barns burned to the ground.

7

j 7 j7 17 71 177 771 1771 7717 7171 1717 177 771 17 71 7jj7
He has 177 pennies, 171 nickels, 77 dimes, and 71 quarters.
777 j7j7j j7j The 77 cars averaged 77.7 mph for 77 minutes.
The 71 settlers and the 17 animals arrived here about 1771.

8

k 8 k8 18 81 188 881 1881 8818 8181 1818 188 881 18 81 8kk8
She has 8 hats, 18 skirts, 18 dresses, 8 suits, and 1 coat.
888 k8k8k k8k The 88 pianists pounded 88 keys on 88 pianos.
He bought 81 pounds of number 18 nails on October 18, 1881.

9

1 9 19 19 91 199 991 1991 9919 9191 1919 199 991 19 91 9119
They sold him 9 chairs, 19 tables, 91 lamps, and 119 desks.
999 19191 191 The 99th Regiment sent 99 men for 99 parades.
The new school holds 919 students; the older one, 991 more.

0

; 0 ;0 10 01 100 001 1001 0010 0101 1010 100 001 10 01 0;;0
There are 1,010 creeks, 110 rivers, and 100 lakes up there.
000 ;0;0; ;0; The 100 girls had scores between 100 and 110.
They gave 1,010 persons 1,100 promissory notes in 100 days.

1 Pamela works for us but may wish to work for the city firm.
2 When did he go to the city and pay them for the world maps?
3 They may make a big profit if they work with the field men.

4 The goal of the rich man is to fix a bicycle for the girls.
5 He and I did work the eighth problem also, and it is right.
6 He paid the neighbor to make an ivory panel for the chapel.

7 When did she go to the man and pay for the Oak Lake island?
8 To make it to town, I paid a neighbor to sit with the girl.
9 The name of the firm they own is to the right on the forms.

10 If the men do their work by six, they may go to the social.
11 The profit on eighty bushels of corn may pay for the chair.
12 Rickey did not wish to pay the usual duty for the fur pelt.

13 They may end the big fight by the lake by the usual signal.
14 I am to go to work for the audit firm by the eighth of May.
15 Their men wish to blame me for both of their big work jams.

NUMBER REVIEW

**The only way to master number keys is through repetitive practice.
Keep your eyes on the copy and use the correct fingering.**

Line: 60
Spacing: Single

1

aqa aqlqa ala ala l ll lll la lla al aal ala lal ala lal al
The 11 men won 111 prizes in 11 games and 11 in 111 others.
He has seat 1 in car 1 of train 1, which is now at gate 11.

2

s 2 s2 12 21 122 221 1221 2212 2121 1212 122 221 12 21 2ss2
Send them 22 tablets, 22 pencils, 22 books, and 22 erasers.
222 s2s2s s2s The 22 men got 22 tickets for the 2:22 train.
Send 12 to us, 21 to Joan, 22 to Richard, and 211 to Grace.

3

d 3 d3 13 31 133 331 1331 3313 3131 1313 133 331 13 31 3dd3
She saw 33 towns, 31 villages, 313 cities, and 13 counties.
333 d3d3d d3d The 33 boys had 33 books with 33 stamps each.
The hotel lost 31 sheets or towels in 3 months and 13 days.

4

f 4 f4 14 41 144 441 1441 4414 4141 1414 144 441 14 41 4ff4
The dates are: May 14, 1444; May 4, 1441; and May 4, 1414.
444 f4f4f f4f The 44 dogs had 44 collars with 44 gold tags.
The law was passed on June 14, 1141, not November 14, 1441.

5

f 5 f5 15 51 155 551 1551 5515 5151 1515 155 551 15 51 5ff5
It took 5 months, 5 weeks, 5 days, 5 hours, and 15 minutes.
555 f5f5f f5f The 55 men checked 55 references in 55 books.
She sold 115 in April, 151 in May, and 155 or more in June.

1 Henry did cut the eye a bit and may go to the city for aid.
2 Alene got a giant fish for the dog and paid me for the box.
3 Dick paid their firm to handle the audit forms for the men.

4 Three or four maps go to the members of the downtown panel.
5 The neighbor may cut the hay for them if the land is right.
6 Jane's neighbor kept the dog and also paid for the big pen.

7 He and Jay may aid the man and cut the hay for the big cow.
8 He did fix the pen for the sow and may bid for the big tub.
9 The coal firm also pays them when they unload the material.

10 Rodney signs the eight forms when the usual audit is right.
11 The chairperson of their committee will handle the problem.
12 The duty they paid irks them when they work with such risk.

13 Both the firm and the city own the property near the river.
14 The widow is kept busy with the field and turkeys she owns.
15 The men may fix their antique auto and go downtown with it.

Use **F** finger.   Use **J** finger.

Read the paragraph and then keyboard a copy.

Goal: Lines 14-16 in 1 minute (26 words) with 2 or fewer errors. If goal is not achieved, repeat this page.

A. LOCATION DRILLS

1 f55f f55f f5f5 f5f5 5 falls 5 fires 5 folks 5 red
2 55 fell 55 find 55 fewer 55 fix 55 fuss 5/55 5:55
3 jy6j jy6j j66j j6j6 6 jays 6 jumps 6 jugs 6 jades
4 66 join 66 jump 66 more 66 must 66 have 1/66 1:16

B. SENTENCES

5 The answer to No. 155 is either 55 1/2 or 55 2/5.
6 We shall need 666 pencils and 66 pens for 66 men.
7 She asked for rooms 55 and 66; he rang 56 and 65.

C. KEYBOARDING CONCEPTS: *Formatting*

8   The keyboard operator can establish the for-
9 mat of the data for printing. This includes such
10 things as line spacing, page size, and margins.
11 This information is stored on magnetic media for
12 recall later. When the data is recalled, it will
13 appear in the format established by the operator.

D. PROGRESS CHECK

14 The warehouse cannot fill our company's order for
15 5 cartons of typing elements or 6 cases of carbon
16 paper until later in the week.

NUMBERS

Other keyboards are designed so that numbers can be keyboarded with selected right-hand alphabetic keys when the machine is set in the numeric mode.

Most keyboards have a row of numbers from 1 through 9 or 0 across the top of the keyboard above the three alphabetic rows.

Some keyboards also have a separate or auxiliary number pad similar to that of a 10-key calculator.

The three basic types of number keyboards are show above. (A special section for developing skill on a 10-key device begins on page 60.)

Use ; finger.

Read the paragraph and then keyboard a copy.

Goal: Lines 14-16 in 1 minute (26 words) with 2 or fewer errors. If goal is not achieved, repeat this page.

A. LOCATION DRILLS

1 ;$\frac{1}{2}\frac{1}{2}$; ;$\frac{1}{2}\frac{1}{2}$; ;$\frac{1}{2}$;$\frac{1}{2}$;$\frac{1}{2}$;$\frac{1}{2}$ $\frac{1}{2}$ pay; $\frac{1}{2}$ mile; $\frac{1}{2}$ hour; $\frac{1}{2}$ week
2 Yes, 4 is $\frac{1}{2}$ of 8, 4$\frac{1}{2}$ is $\frac{1}{2}$ of 9, and 7 is $\frac{1}{2}$ of 14.
3 ;$\frac{1}{2}\frac{1}{4}$; ;$\frac{1}{2}\frac{1}{4}$; ;$\frac{1}{4}$;$\frac{1}{4}$;$\frac{1}{4}$;$\frac{1}{4}$ $\frac{1}{4}$ pay; $\frac{1}{4}$ mile; $\frac{1}{4}$ hour; $\frac{1}{4}$ week
4 Yes, 2 is $\frac{1}{4}$ of 8, 2$\frac{1}{4}$ is $\frac{1}{4}$ of 9, and 7 is $\frac{1}{4}$ of 28.

B. SENTENCES

5 He worked 10$\frac{1}{2}$ hours in May and 11$\frac{1}{2}$ hours in June.
6 We gave $\frac{1}{2}$ to him and $\frac{1}{4}$ to her; I got the other $\frac{1}{4}$.
7 When she added $\frac{1}{2}$ and $\frac{1}{4}$ and 1$\frac{1}{4}$ and 2$\frac{1}{2}$, she got 4$\frac{1}{2}$.

C. KEYBOARDING CONCEPTS: *Function Keys*

8   Function keys on a keyboard activate signals
9 not associated with a printable character. When
10 a signal is detected, the system is able to per-
11 form a predefined function. Examples of commonly
12 used function keys are the return key, the delete
13 key, the index key, and the stop key.

D. PROGRESS CHECK

14 They were very excited and amazed when the broker
15 quoted the jump of only $\frac{1}{4}$ or $\frac{1}{2}$ for that preferred
16 stock that I bought last week.

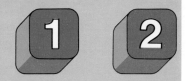

Use A finger. Use S finger.

SHIFT ⬛ SHIFT

Read the paragraph and then keyboard a copy.

Indent 5 spaces for a paragraph.

Note: If there is no 1 key on the machine you are using, use the L key.

Goal: Lines 15-17 in 1 minute (22 words) with 2 or fewer errors. If goal is not achieved, repeat this page.

A. LOCATION DRILLS

1 aqla aqla alla alla alal alal all lll and lll,lll
2 ll arts ll axes ll aims ll alms ll aces l.ll l:ll
3 sw2s sw2s s22s s22s s2s2 s2s2 all 222 and ll2,l22
4 22 sons 22 sums 22 seas 22 sips 22 suns 2.22 2:22

B. SENTENCES

5 We need ll pairs of size ll shoes for the ll men.
6 The l2 men and the 22 boys played l22 full games.
7 Of the l22 who paid, only ll or l2 were children.

C. KEYBOARDING CONCEPTS: *Information Processing*

8   The term information processing is used to
9 describe the integration of data processing, word
10 processing, reprographics, and records manage—
11 ment. It includes all business and scientific
12 operations performed by computer, such as han—
13 dling, merging, sorting, computing, and editing
14 data.

D. PROGRESS CHECK

15 Jenny was amazed to see the l2 new terminals. It
16 will be very quiet for the group in the back room
17 next week.

Use **L** finger. Use **;** finger.

SHIFT   SHIFT

Read the paragraph and then keyboard a copy.

Goal: Lines 15-17 in 1 minute (24 words) with 2 or fewer errors. If goal is not achieved, repeat this page.

A. LOCATION DRILLS

1 lo91 lo91 1991 1991 1919 1919 all 999 for 234,789
2 99 lots 99 lids 99 laws 99 logs 99 less 9/19 9:19
3 ;p0; ;p0; ;00; ;00; ;0;0 ;0;0 dip 000 for 347,890
4 10 pegs 10 pins 10 play 10 paid 10 push 1/10 1:10

B. SENTENCES

5 In 1919, there were 199 men in each of 19 lodges.
6 She saw 1,000 horses in those 100 pens at 10 a.m.
7 The 90 men and 90 boys ate 90 apples and 90 pies.

C. KEYBOARDING CONCEPTS: Memory

8   The memory is a component of information
9 processing systems where data are stored. It
10 may be an internal part of the system or in the
11 form of removable media such as cards, tapes, or
12 disks. Information being entered, edited, or
13 formatted is stored in the memory for later
14 retrieval.

D. PROGRESS CHECK

15 They acquired 90 vacant lots. We will extend the
16 residential zone for one-family dwellings to just
17 beyond the new park.

Use **D** finger. Use **F** finger.

SHIFT   SHIFT

Read the paragraph and then keyboard a copy.

Goal: Lines 14-16 in 1 minute (22 words) with 2 or fewer errors. If goal is not achieved, repeat this page.

A. LOCATION DRILLS

1 de3d de3d d33d d33d d3d3 d3d3 all 333 and 123,123
2 33 dads 33 dips 33 dues 33 dots 33 dogs 3.13 3:13
3 fr4f fr4f f44f f44f f4f4 f4f4 all 444 and 123,441
4 44 furs 44 fins 44 fish 44 fell 44 flew 4.14 4:14

B. SENTENCES

5 Did the 3 men catch 31 or 33 fish in the 13 days?
6 The 44 boys lost only 14 of their 144 golf games.
7 All of the 34 companies asked to buy our produce.

C. KEYBOARDING CONCEPTS: Input/Output

8   Input is the process of entering information
9 into a system for processing. The keyboard is a
10 common method of inputting. Output is the final
11 result produced by a system after recorded input
12 is processed, revised, or printed out. The terms
13 also refer to the information itself.

D. PROGRESS CHECK

14 Vi had 3 or 4 extra plants, too many for the size
15 of the rooms. The janitor will seek to acquire 2
16 big rooms.

Use J finger. Use K finger.

Read the paragraph and then keyboard a copy.

Goal: Lines 15-17 in 1 minute (24 words) with 2 or fewer errors. If goal is not achieved, repeat this page.

A. LOCATION DRILLS

1 ju7j ju7j j77j j77j j7j7 j7j7 you 777 for 123,477
2 77 jugs 77 jars 77 jigs 77 jets 77 jogs 7/17 7:17
3 ki8k ki8k k88k k88k k8k8 k8k8 irk 888 for 123,478
4 88 kits 88 keys 88 kids 88 inks 88 inns 8/18 8:18

B. SENTENCES

5 On June 7, the 7 men left Camp 7 on the 7:17 bus.
6 Train No. 188 departs at 11:18 a.m. or 12:18 p.m.
7 Of the 178 who paid, only 37 or 38 were children.

C. KEYBOARDING CONCEPTS: Printer

8   The printer may be an integral part of a
9 keyboard or a separate unit wired to the key-
10 board. An impact printer uses an element which
11 strikes the paper directly to produce characters,
12 while the ink-jet printer sprays ink through an
13 electrostatic field and onto paper to form the
14 characters.

D. PROGRESS CHECK

15 Their quota will be increased to 7 dozen from the
16 78 set earlier. This goes beyond the old goal by
17 exactly six packets.